# JOSEPH SOBRAN

# The *National Review* Years

# Books by Joseph Sobran:

*Alias Shakespeare: Solving the Greatest Literary Mystery of All Time* (The Free Press, a division of Simon & Schuster, 1997)

*Shakespeare Explained* series:
*Hamlet* (2008); and *Julius Caesar* (2009), published by Marshall Cavendish Children's Books.
*A Midsummer Night's Dream* (2009); *Henry IV, Part I* (2009-2010); and *Twelfth Night* (2009-2010) published by Marshall Cavendish Benchmark Books

Collections of Joseph Sobran's writings

*Single Issues: Essays on the Crucial Social Questions* (The Human Life Press, 1983) Compiled by Joseph Sobran. Introduction by J.P. McFadden

*Hustler: The Clinton Legacy* (first edition, Griffin Communications, 2000; second edition, FGF Books, 2016) Edited by Tom McPherren. Foreword by Ann Coulter

*Anything Called a Program is Unconstitutional: Confessions of a Reactionary Utopian* (Griffin Communications, 2001) — booklet of quotations taken from *Sobran's: The Real News of the Month*

*Regime Change Begins At Home:*
*Confessions of a Reactionary Utopian*
(Griffin Communications, 2006) — booklet of quotations taken from *Sobran's: The Real News of the Month*

*Subtracting Christianity: Essays on American Culture and Society* (FGF Books, 2015) Edited by Fran Griffin and Tom Bethell. Preface by Most Rev. Fabian W. Bruskewitz. Foreword by Rev. J.J. Pokorsky

# JOSEPH SOBRAN

# The *National Review* Years

*Articles from 1974 to 1991*

## Joseph Sobran

Fran Griffin
Editor

Foreword by Patrick J. Buchanan
Preface by Tom Bethell
Afterword by Ann Coulter

FGF Books
PUBLISHING IMPRINT OF
Fitzgerald Griffin Foundation
VIENNA, VIRGINIA

Foreword by Patrick J. Buchanan, Preface by Tom Bethell, Introduction by Fran Griffin, Afterword by Ann Coulter, cover design, formatting, design, and typesetting copyright © 2017 by FGF Books, the publishing imprint of the Fitzgerald Griffin Foundation. Text of Sobran articles copyright *National Review*. All rights reserved. No part of this book may be used or reproduced in any manner without permission in writing from the Fitzgerald Griffin Foundation except in the case of brief quotations in books, articles or reviews.

Typesetting and design by the St. Martin de Porres Lay Dominican Community, New Hope, Kentucky.

Cover design by John Frantz

The photo on page 147 is a copy of a *National Review* magazine cover from June 11, 1990. It depicts Joe Sobran in a New York Yankees uniform at Yankee Stadium to illustrate his article, "Take Me Out to the Ballgame: The Republic of Baseball." The text to the right of his picture reads, "*NR*'s Slugger Joe Sobran."

*JOSEPH SOBRAN*
*The National Review Years*
*Articles from 1974 to 1991*
ISBN-13: 978-1548513405
ISBN-10: 1548513407

*Second Edition, 2017*

Fitzgerald Griffin Foundation
344 Maple Avenue West, #281
Vienna, Virginia 22180-5612
www.fgfBooks.com

*Dedicated to the loyal supporters of Joe Sobran, and to future generations of Sobran readers. May his words and wisdom inspire many for years to come.*

# Contents

| | |
|---|---|
| Foreword by Patrick J. Buchanan | xi |
| Preface by Tom Bethell | xv |
| Introduction by Fran Griffin | xvii |
| My Days at *National Review* | 1 |
| Journalism *v.* Conservatism | 4 |
| What Is This Thing Called Sex? | 7 |
| A Nation of Loners | 15 |
| Howard Beach: The Use and Abuse of Race | 20 |
| Writing on the Wall | 30 |
| Piety for the Future | 33 |
| Unbelievers | 36 |
| Rainbow in Central Park | 39 |
| Mavericks in Lockstep | 47 |
| No-Fault Media Bias | 49 |
| Acute Philophilia | 58 |
| The Sage and Serious Doctrine of Hugh Hefner | 61 |
| Gone With the Whip | 69 |
| Mass on the Mall | 72 |
| That *Commonweal* Girl | 75 |
| Memoirs of an Unsung Hero | 78 |
| Those Who Can't | 81 |
| Up to Liberalism | 84 |

| | |
|---|---|
| Martyr-in-Chief | 91 |
| Mindsets | 94 |
| James Burnham, 1905–1987: Editor, Thinker, Colleague | 97 |
| Censorship, Stereotypes, and Other Fine Things | 100 |
| Heirs of Elvis | 111 |
| Stony Rolls | 114 |
| Bard Thou Never Wert | 117 |
| Less Is More | 125 |
| The Lord and the Bard | 128 |
| The Feast of St. Gilbert | 132 |
| Olivier | 135 |
| A Fair Shake for Oxford | 138 |
| Priest Bites Bishop | 141 |
| The Republic of Baseball | 146 |
| Choosing Death | 156 |
| Afterword by Ann Coulter | 159 |
| Biographical Sketch of Joseph Sobran | 165 |
| Sobran Book Benefactors | 167 |
| Index | 169 |
| Fitzgerald Griffin Foundation | 193 |

# Foreword

To reread the essays in *Joseph Sobran: The National Review Years* is to appreciate anew the loss that the conservative cause and his friends suffered when Joe passed away, too young, in September 2010.

His voice was unique, his style readily identifiable, his wit irrepressible, his range as wide as that of any columnist of his generation. In one of the first essays in this volume, a retrospective on Woodstock 20 years later, one has only to stumble across the first lines to recognize the familiar voice:

"The entire hippie economy was based on freeloading...."

"To give you some idea of how unstructured Woodstock was, Abbie Hoffman was partially responsible for security."

Joe made us laugh out loud at the pretentiousness of it all. And, for all the media chatter about Woodstock auguring "a new value system that could change (for the better, of course) the American national character," Joe saw it for what it was — a pathetic gathering of half-a-million loners and losers for a weekend of sex, drugs, rock, and a sense of belonging.

They would be called Woodstock Nation and would be celebrated as the apotheosis of the counterculture. And how did it all end?

"Several of the rockers who performed at Woodstock [Janis Joplin, Jimi Hendrix] have died, most of them from drug overdoses. Abbie Hoffman, who resurfaced after ten years on the lam for a cocaine rap, killed himself in April...."

"Another glory of Woodstock, free love, has also come a cropper.... Like drugs, it has been a source of personal and social devastation.... The destruction has been worst in the chief target of liberal solicitude, the black inner city. Dionysus has worn out his welcome."

In the book's longest essay, "Howard Beach: The Use and Abuse of Race," Joe recognizes and reveals the taproot of the famous "media bias" that so distorts the journalism of our day.

What happened at Howard Beach was scarcely unusual. Three tough mean kids tried to beat up a stranger in their neighborhood. He ran from them into traffic, and was killed.

A brutal act, but hardly one that would have seized the attention not only of Queens, where it occurred, but also of the national journalistic community.

Why did it garner such attention? Because the victim was black and the thugs white.

Behind the small story, writes Joe, lies the "super-story," the dark myth about America that is a preexisting condition in the minds of reporters who compulsively search for events and episodes to confirm that myth.

Though Howard Beach was untypical of most interracial assaults, it was a perfect exhibit for helping to prove an indictment against an America long ago convicted of racism in the minds of media elites. Writes Joe: "The media are so saturated with myth that it's fair to see 'news' as an early stage on the assembly line whose final product is a *New York Times* editorial." Journalists sort out from the myriad events that daily occur those which conform to their preconceived view of the society and nation in which they live.

In "Martyr-in-Chief" on Carter vs. Reagan, written only a month after Reagan took his oath, Joe captured the essence of why Carter had failed and why Reagan would succeed in the struggle between the media and the Right.

"Intellectuals who live by playing up their intelligence don't understand Reagan. He lives by playing his down. He… has a genius for empathy; he can reach people, putting his thoughts in their language. To call him simplistic is simply simplistic."

No collection of Joe's essays would be complete without one or two devoted to the cause of life and another few selections highlighting the literary cause of Joe's career: establishing the Earl of Oxford as the true author of the Shakespearean plays and sonnets Joe knew as well as any scholar of English literature.

Joe had a fine reporter's ear. Confessing that he had quietly and closely studied his eldest colleague at *NR*, James Burnham, the former Trotskyist turned Cold War geostrategist, Joe went to Burnham's office after a "State Department official had announced, with moral pomp, that the U.S. was withdrawing recognition of Rhodesia."

"I found Jim alone… on a quiet midsummer day. He commented, 'Sometimes, in this world, you have to throw your friends to the wolves. But you don't have to talk a lot of s--- about democracy when you do it.'"

From these few words that Joe extracted from him, one learns much about Burnham: He saw white-ruled Rhodesia as part of the West, a friend in the larger struggle. He understood the awful imperative of sometimes having to abandon one's friends. He had contempt for the liberal belief in the moral superiority of majority rule and one-man, one-vote democracy.

Again, what is extraordinary about this book of essays is the range of Joe's interests and the quality of his insights. It reminds us why we so miss his commentary — and his company.

*Pat Buchanan*
*May 2012*

# Preface

I first met Joe Sobran in 1980 and we became close friends from that time. His literary ability, his originality, learning, eloquence, and the sheer speed with which he could produce articles reached the level of genius. I never saw anything like it. I once tested him on his claim to know the whole of Shakespeare by heart. He had the *Collected Works* in his car, the back seat crammed full of newspapers and other junk right up to the rear window. I flipped through the volume, taking care not to let him see the particular play. I would read a line at random, and his task was to say the next line. I did it five or six times and he got it right every time.

Sometimes, in his rented house in Arlington, Virginia, I would see him produce a newspaper column in half an hour on an electric typewriter perched on a wobbly Formica-topped table. The entire ground floor of the house would be ankle-deep in what an admirer once called a "landfill." His column would materialize with no corrections. "Order from chaos," as Matthew Scully wrote, in his great testimonial to Joe published by *National Review.*

Joe learned to use a computer — with Bill Buckley's encouragement and assistance — and the new machine was helpful enough to give Joe the burst of energy he needed to complete *Alias Shakespeare: Solving The Greatest Literary Mystery of All Time,* his one book-length work. Otherwise I believe all his columns and articles were written in a single sitting. If he had to return to something, he would inevitably have lost the first draft somewhere in the landfill, so he would start over from the beginning.

I'm told he joined *National Review* on 9/11/71. Old hands at the magazine have good stories about Joe in those years. In learning his Shakespeare, they say, he never had to work at it. It just stayed with him once he read it. We tend to call such rare people geniuses. Perhaps a more realistic definition of genius is "an infinite capacity to take pains." That was not Joe!

He was the intellectual equivalent of a natural athlete who can reach Olympic standards with no training. Later, as he puts on a few years and a few pounds, the athlete loses it and he has no discipline or good habits to fall back on. That is what happened to Joe, more or less. His great gift began to fade. Then he had to make big efforts to do what he once did effortlessly.

Often, Joe seemed to have little understanding of the quality of his own writing and he quickly forgot what he had written. It's as though he was a mere conduit through which his genius was transmitted.

An old friend of Joe's, a sweet guy from Michigan called Bob Maday, would come to Washington and they would go book-hunting together. (I am glad to say that Joe donated most of his books, including an outstanding Shakespeare collection, to Christendom College in Front Royal, Virginia.) Bob once said that Joe "won't be appreciated until he's been dead for a while." That was perceptive.

At its best, Joe's writing was better organized than G.K Chesterton's. Anyway, here are some of his *National Review* articles, and the good news is that there's enough material from other publications for a couple more books.

Michael Joseph Sobran, 1946-2010, R.I.P.

*Tom Bethell*
*Senior Editor of* The American Spectator

# Introduction

One day I was listening to the local radio news station in my hometown of Chicago and heard a magnificent baritone voice expounding many of the same ideas I had. It turned out to be Joe Sobran giving one of his commentaries on "CBS Spectrum." I was intrigued — and pleased to hear such a rational voice on the air.

Not too long afterward, at a 1980 meeting of the Philadelphia Society, I met him for the first time. Joe was then a senior editor for *National Review* and a syndicated columnist for the Los Angeles Times Syndicate. His column was carried in major newspapers throughout the country, including even *The Philadelphia Inquirer* and *The Washington Post*! For many years his voice was heard on the CBS Spectrum series by millions of people throughout the country. He was giving speeches at many events in the U.S. and abroad. Yet to encounter Joe Sobran was to be with a man who was witty, engaging, and not caught up with a sense of his own self-importance. He had perfect timing when telling jokes, which he loved to do, and he had quite a repertoire of them. A brilliant conversationalist, Joe loved to expound on politics, religion, sports, current events, books, movies, classical music, and even singers (Sinatra was one of his favorites). He read for hours and hours every day and seemed to know something about almost everything! What everyone who knew him soon discovered is that Joe usually had a unique insight on almost any topic that was being discussed.

My everyday involvement with Joe began shortly after he left *National Review*. He asked me to partner with him on a joint venture: a monthly newsletter. The first issue *of Sobran's: The Real News of the Month* came out in September 1994, and the newsletter was, by the grace of God, published nearly every month for the next 13 years. He was the editor; I was the publisher. It was a terrific newsletter in which Joe, at last, did not feel constrained by pesky editors. In fact, our loyal newsletter managing editor, Ronald Neff, had very little editing to do, as Joe's copy was almost flawless.

It was sometime during the years that I was publisher of *Sobran's* that a very large padded envelope — with at least a ream of paper in it — unexpectedly arrived at my office. It contained a collection of

Sobran articles that had been selected by the *National Review* staff. Joe explained that these articles had been chosen by the magazine to be published in a book. However, after he left *NR*, the publishing project never saw the light of day. An encouraging letter that accompanied the articles suggested that this collection be published. As people learned of its existence, they urged me to organize it into a book.

In the meantime, one of Joe's loyal friends and a huge fan of his writing, Patricia Alvarez (1952-2008), spent hours at the Library of Congress, going through every issue of *National Review* from 1971 to 1993, looking for Sobran columns. During her lunch hour and after work, she copied from microfilm every article that Joe had written for the magazine. Then one day she arrived with two boxes containing every by-lined word that Sobran had written for *National Review*.

In late 2003, the Fitzgerald Griffin Foundation was founded. Joe and Sam Francis were our first two resident scholars. I started thinking about publishing the *NR* collection, but knew that it would be a massive task to complete. With the encouragement of Joe's close friend, Tom Bethell, along with donors to the foundation, this publishing project has finally seen the light of day.

None of the columns was digitalized. All had to be converted to text by either scanning or typing. This volume contains many of the *NR* articles originally selected by the magazine for publication. But it also includes additional pieces that I found when I began reading the material amassed by Patricia Alvarez. This first collection since his untimely passing two years ago showcases Joe's thinking from the early days at *National Review* magazine until his last years there.

I hope you find it to be an exhilarating read.

As with any project of this magnitude, many people were involved. Tom Bethell, a great friend of Joe's who emigrated from Great Britain in 1962, was certainly a catalyst. I have lost track of how many times he urged me to publish this book. He also carefully reviewed every article and made many valuable suggestions, as well as contributing the Preface.

Br. Mario Calabrese, O.P. and Fr. Ronald Tacelli, S.J. also read over the many articles selected for the book and made recommendations as to what should be included. Rick Docksai went to the

Library of Congress to check on dates and titles of some of the articles as well as typing and proofing many pages and providing editorial assistance. Alan Potter and Nona Aguilar both made important editorial suggestions. The St. Martin de Porres Lay Dominican Community in New Hope, Kentucky, scanned hundreds of pages of articles, converted them to text, and typeset and laid out the book. Ann Brown proofread every article against the original documents, and then proofed it a few more times. John Frantz designed the beautiful cover. Susan Roberson, the long-time office manager and bookkeeper for FGF Books, helped in numerous ways to push the project to completion.

I am grateful to Pat Buchanan for his excellent Foreword and to Ann Coulter for her lively, entertaining Afterword.

Our magnanimous donors made it possible for us to get this book produced. I am very thankful for the generous donations by the loyal Sobran brigade. We have dedicated a page of this book to these wonderful souls (see page 167). We do not have the space to list every donor to this project, as there have been over 100 of them, some giving their widow's mite to preserve Sobran's legacy. You would not be reading this book if it were not for all of our donors, big and small.

Last but not least, I am indebted to my dear friend of three decades, Joe Sobran, for penning such magnificent articles. I hope they will be an inspiration for many generations to come.

*Fran Griffin, President*
*Fitzgerald Griffin Foundation*

# My Days At *National Review*

*December 19, 1975*

As *NR* was observing its twentieth anniversary as a magazine, I was observing my tenth as its reader. I was a college student in 1965 when I picked up my first copy of *NR* and awoke from my dogmatic slumber. Though naturally of a conservative disposition, I had been taught to think that enlightened political opinion was, as one of my teachers had discreetly told me, "a little bit pinkish." I had accepted this as one of those oppressive facts of life, and left the whole subject of politics to those possessed of that strange appetite for banality, while I frolicked away my youth in the embrace of Shakespeare.

How liberating, then, to find this little magazine, so bright and literate and pungent, speaking of politics, and even of politicians, as if they were interesting. And by the mass, they *were* interesting! What a shock to find the subject treated in something besides the familiar bland editorialese, that monotonous incantation of the Great Sect of our time, whose high-minded votaries are so soothing in their indignation, so alarming in their reassurances. No, here was prose full of real anger and laughter, both fused in wit, softened by charity and self-mockery. Who but *NR*'s editors would begin the first issue after Kennedy's murder by announcing, regretfully, that their patience with President Lyndon Johnson was exhausted? How restorative; how gracious.

Perhaps the point is best made by contrast with another magazine whose excellence I toast. In many ways no finer magazine than *Commentary* exists. Yet it has the defects of its virtues, summed up bluntly by friends of mine (who read both magazines faithfully) in the word "humorless." The tone is a little too solemn and troubled — not because Mr. Podhoretz has forgot to include cartoons and party jokes, but because his magazine is devoted to what are called *ideas* and *issues*. Its conservatism, so to call it, is entirely thoughtful, because it is (or presents itself as) entirely thought: all reasoned, deduced, concluded, what Newman called notional. It aims at unexceptionable abstractions — a worthy aspiration — and it achieves them. At its high level of generality, with the aid of very little earthiness, it absorbs and edifies.

But *National Review* was always fun. Fun because its approach is *real,* rather than merely notional. Its conservatism has always attached to things, people, places, facts. Not that it has lacked ideas; it has always offered the sublimer pleasure too, what with contributors like Willmoore Kendall, James Burnham, Milton Friedman, Ernest van den Haag, and others whose gifts for sheer analysis remind us that thought itself is an adventure. Still, *NR*'s chief virtue has always seemed to me its courage in standing its ground even when the authoritative ideas of the day were against it. ("Ideas" has in fact become a tendentious term: as in "persecution of ideas," which generally means "hostility to liberalism.")

If a fanatic is a man who redoubles his efforts when he has forgotten his reasons, *NR* was willing to persist in its efforts before its reasons were fully explicit, while much of the world denied there were any reasons. Its conservatism was frankly rooted in concrete and local things, addressed with love and loyalty, faith and habit, piety and prepossession. *Commentary* has always reasoned intelligently, but so have the men who have done the great mischief of this century. *NR* has been wise enough to see and feel and taste intelligently as well — even to laugh and curse intelligently. Never for a moment has it affected the posture of those who seem to have been made by some other deity than Nature. It knew, and knew instantly: that, for instance, Eleanor Roosevelt was funny, and that Joseph Stalin was a monster. It knew *why* she was funny and he monstrous; but it knew *that* before it knew *why,* and proceeded always on the sane assumption that *that* came before *why.* One might almost say it took its bearings from its jokes. In this direct and hearty response to reality, it proved that it really was conservative; which the liberals proved again by complaining that it really wasn't conservative. (Only liberalism, you know, is really conservative.)

"When speculation has done its worst," says Dr. Johnson, "two and two still make four." The vital thing about *NR* was that sentiment, boldly asserted without reference to whether it had been vindicated once and for all by Russell and Whitehead. And *NR* stood up to defend the West in the same spirit: liberty was under attack and deserved our devotion and protection whether or not this was admitted in enlightened circles. When the tenured heretics of the day were unanimously propagating the certitude that nothing is certain, a despised little party rose to mutiny for orthodoxy. And they have been partly rewarded: though these things are never settled, a great deal of speculation has tended to vindicate them — as has a great deal of the history they stood athwart. The missionary ambitions of states have produced ruin, confusion, oppression. Communism has refused to let itself be domesticated. The United Nations has sunk to a degree of perversity that embarrasses even its warmest advocates of yesteryear. Democratic welfarism has debased currencies, inflamed appetites, increased dissension and discontent. Arthur Schlesinger has given up on the Presidency.

Ah, yes. Arthur Schlesinger. Mrs. Roosevelt. Chester Bowles. Harriet Van Horne. Hubert Humphrey. Bella Abzug. These are but a few of the characters whose antic utterances have so enlivened *NR*'s pages these last twenty years. Should a magazine be "above" personalities? Heaven forbid. Apart from the fun of running gags, it is instructive to see such exemplars of right thinking — who, after all, trade heavily on reputation and personal authority (and who comment acidly enough on those who oppose them) — deflated. For all the cant about "openness to ideas" (that word again!), they cooperate to impose an ersatz consensus on the rest of us. It is interesting that four of the largest publications in the country, *Reader's Digest*, *TV Guide*, the *Wall Street Journal*, and the *New York Daily News*, are all staunchly conservative — and all lie outside the great liberal System of Mutual Quotation, by which the respectable fictions of the day are established and sustained. The great achievement of *National Review* has been to juxtapose this System and its spokesmen with the real world. That is why reading *NR* has always given me a hilarious sense of liberation; why it so keenly mortifies others; and why there is probably no other magazine in America so loved and hated.

# Journalism *v.* Conservatism

*November 5, 1990*

Words seem to form partnerships. At one time, you discriminated *between*. Now you discriminate *against*. "Discrimination" now betokens not a fine mind, but a character flaw: one that makes you Politically Incorrect, by the way.

Liberalism has succeeded in imposing its verbal prescriptions on the whole population: everyone must now mind even his or her pronouns, or face obloquy. Politesse has shifted from "Negro" to "black" to "African-American," each new whim of whoever decides these things as imperious as the last. A sectarian ideology has triumphed when it has turned itself into an etiquette that all must observe.

We all sense that the language has been marshaled into Political Correctness. Is there any central ordering principle?

I think so. It was expressed succinctly in the chant of the Stanford protestors: "Hey hey, ho ho, Western culture's gotta go." We're being nudged into a series of little repudiations of the Western patrimony. The changing rules embody this. Profanity and obscenity are okay; but new taboos forbid "racism," "sexism," and other Politically Incorrect attitudes. (Religion is purely optional, but bigotry must be "eliminated.")

In *The Whig Interpretation of History,* Herbert Butterfield lamented the tendency of historians to see the controversies of the past in the anachronistic categories of "progressive" and "reactionary": Whig history interpreted the clash of, say, Reformers and Church not in terms the raging opponents would have understood, but as a battle between the forces of the future (Luther) and the forces of the past (Pope Leo X).

This way of flattening complicated disputes into easily grasped melodrama has trickled down into journalism. Many "news" stories have as their subtext the battle between Progressive good guys and Reactionary villains. Despite the official journalistic ethic of neutrality, unmistakable moral commitment creeps into news reports of conflict between pope and theologian, government and protestor, business and labor, white and black, male and female. We sense we're getting cues as to which side we should be rooting for.

The Progressive forces are always driven by the best motives: they are compassionate, courageous, conscientious, enlightened, future-oriented, peace-loving. These terms all have a left-wing odor about them now (though the media rarely use the term "left-wing"). The Reactionaries, meanwhile, are driven by atavisms: hate, fear, superstition, greed, ignorance, selfishness, sheer resistance to "change."

"Hate," for example, has become associated exclusively with "right-wing" causes in journalistic discourse. (See *Newsweek,* passim.) No Progressive ever *hates* anyone, though he (or she) may feel righteous *anger* or *rage*. Journalese does use the term "right-wing" freely, but without defining it: it is a catchall for anything belonging to the dark past. Theocracy, capitalism, slavery, militarism: these are right wing. The fascist, the monarchist, the libertarian, the constitutionalist: all, somehow, right wing, though their only common denominator is that they all oppose socialism.

What conservatives call "bias" in the media is really more like a *Weltanschauung,* half-conscious, but shaping and shading everything. Journalists may try hard to be accurate and to suppress overt partisanship; they usually don't realize they are taking sides in the very categories they start with. They don't understand that there are alternative categories.

**Behind the Times**

In the mind of the thoroughly assimilated journalist, the conservative is not someone who has a specific philosophy to be discussed, listened to, debated. He's simply someone who's behind the times, clinging to the disreputable and embarrassing past that all educated people should have outgrown. The conservative is not so much wrong as defunct, doomed to extinction. Why debate a dinosaur?

The ultimate Progressive categories are not heaven and hell, or good and evil, or order and chaos, but Future and Past. Even the cusswords of the Progressive are chronological: archaic, outdated, Neanderthal, medieval, antediluvian, fossilized, obsolete, mossbound, prehistoric, antiquated, troglodytic, thirteenth- (or eighteenth-) century, etc. To the liberal these are ultimate condemnations, unanswerable. The Past, him bad!

So for the dramaturgy of journalism, the problem in every controversy is a simple matter of typecasting: Which side represents the Past, and which the Future? And this sort of stereotyping, with its built-in predictions as to who's bound to prevail, has led journalists into a series of embarrassing errors. Reagan was Reactionary; therefore he was not a viable candidate. The pro-life movement was Reactionary; therefore it wasn't news (unlike, say, the civil-rights movement). The Shah of Iran and Somoza were Reactionary; therefore they were bound to be supplanted by Progressive forces. (And what do you do with phenomena like 2 Live Crew, which represents free speech — Progressive — but is horribly sexist — Reactionary?)

History itself has begun to demolish the Progressive mythology. Socialism is in moral, political, and economic ruins. The noble savages of the Third World have shown us what comes after "liberation." And it's all so tiresome. We have seen the Future, and it has acquired its own discreditable past. Progressive hope is just about used up. But journalism hasn't yet learned any other language.

# What Is This Thing Called Sex?

*December 31, 1980*

The two great institutions of the twentieth century are Socialism and Sex. Neither is anything to be proud of: one may as well say it. But to say it offends the official and quasi-official etiquettes of good cheer that attend both.

In America you can still denounce Socialism. Under its own name it has even less appeal now than it used to have. It has to be smuggled into the forum these days — under cover of terms like "reindustrialization" and "compassion" that conceal that you are talking about state control. Most people still agree with Oscar Wilde that Socialism would consume too many evenings — one of Wilde's few normal reactions to anything.

But his objection doesn't seem to apply to Sex. Citizens of the free countries think that's what evenings are for. As in Socialist countries you may maintain indifference to Socialism as long as you don't oppose it, so in the West you don't have to have Sex: you only mustn't oppose it. If you do you won't be sent to a camp, but you will face the disguised opprobrium of a diagnosis: the judgment that you lack the capacity, poor fellow, for a wholesome animal *joie de vivre*.

What is this thing called Sex? The indispensable word "sex" has been around for a long long time, but it always meant gender. Then, early in this century, as nearly as I can judge, it came to mean what the sexes do in bed, then it widened to include what two members of one sex do in bed, then what one member of one sex does in bed. This usage would seem as odd to the ribald Donne as to the chaste Tennyson. What we call Sex comes down to any form of genital stimulation.

The act of love has always had a variety of names, full of moral tonalities. And the most comprehensive words, the lowest common denominator of the physical act itself, were necessarily the coarsest ones: they obliterated distinctions among the relations of the participants. Only a crude term could give one name to what a man does with his wife and what a man does with a whore. The new sense imparted to the term Sex serves precisely to name the act without moral, aesthetic, or social effect. It is a deliberately clinical and colorless word.

And we are encouraged to give hearty approval to this stripped-down thing. To disapprove, we are cautioned, is prudery. But of course this is false. You can enjoy conjugal love, or for that matter any of the forms of love that used to be called illicit, without giving your assent to the current notion of Sex. True, the prudes do line up on the anti-Sex side; but then, the lechers line up on the other side. That either position draws to itself certain kinds of neurotics tells us nothing useful about the position's merits.

In the recent movie *Time After Time,* H.G. Wells comes via his time machine into present-day San Francisco, where he discovers that the political utopia he envisioned has failed to come to pass: in its stead, world wars, genocide, endemic crime. It is an amusing, not untender moment of satire. But the film misses a further irony. Wells was also an apostle of "free love." At the beginning of the film he is shown lecturing his friends on this subject as well as Socialism. And surely a man who held that quaint ideal and then abruptly o'erleaped eighty years would notice that the promised erotic utopia too has broken its date with us: in its stead, disease, abortion, the dissolution of loyalties bespoken by illegitimacy and divorce, the neurotic masturbation bespoken by the pornography trade.

And yet we see Wells falling quickly into an affair that effortlessly becomes True Love. This utopia, at least, it's still heresy to doubt. The obligatory Sex scenes are permeated with obligatory false optimism.

A glance over the work of, say, Shakespeare, ought to banish this sentimentalism. The poet with the largest and most comprehensive soul may not supply the detail of Krafft-Ebing, but he does show us a tremendous range of normal human emotions. And love in Shakespeare gives rise to responses that run from ecstatic joy to violent nausea. Romeo and Juliet, Othello and Desdemona, Antony and Cleopatra all harmonize spiritual and carnal love, but the poet gives equal time to the impact of perverse carnality. Othello, Troilus, Posthumus, and Leontes writhe in sick horror even to imagine their lovers' bodies in conjunction with others'. Lear's disgust is more general, a revulsion against lust as such; Hamlet's is more special, when he thinks of his mother and uncle-stepfather, but Horatio doesn't urge him to seek therapy.

Once you recognize as ideal certain forms of love, other things follow. The rival forms may range from imperfect to downright abhorrent. The lasting torment of rape victims, about which we hear so much, ought to prove this. Physically, rape is no worse than a severe beating. But the horror of it lies in a deeper violation than mere pain can inflict. There is something jarring in the contrast between the "trauma" of rape as we hear it described (accurately enough, no doubt) and the general trivialization of Eros. Why in one case alone are we supposed to assume, and accept as normal, that deep nerves are struck? If casual Sex is not to be experienced as defiling, why should a rape seem so lastingly degrading? Do rape victims just happen to be women with more than their share of hangups? Or is it that the experience of rape gives the lie to the ideology of Sex?

## Sanger
*Children as uninvited guests*

Maybe it is our present casualness about Sex that is really artificial. All the propaganda, from Academia to Madison Avenue, stresses only half the truth. We are forever reminded of the beauty and attractiveness of the body. We don't hear (it runs against too many vested interests) of the equally natural modesty and delicacy of the soul, in fact the universal sense of privacy against which all this explicitness batters. Both being natural, we can, if we choose, cultivate the one and coarsen the other. But this is to distort Nature, not to liberate her.

The idea of Sex as a thing existing in abstraction from marriage (or any other specific human connection) came into the popular mind along with the acceptance of contraceptive devices. Hard as it may be to recall, the agitation and scandal of Margaret Sanger's contraception crusade traversed denominational lines; the Catholic Church was only part of the chorus. And as so often happens, the wildest reactionary anxieties were more honest than the soothing promises of reformers: the reactionaries sensed, and warned, that the moral implications of birth control were enormous. When copulation was severed from reproduction, the very essence of the act would be changed. And so it proved. The act became ... Sex.

Contraception was nothing new. Casanova knew about as much on the subject as Mrs. Sanger. David M. Kennedy has noted her tendency to talk as if existing knowledge had been withheld from the public, when in fact you could find it in the public library. She was, in fact, a Socialist ideologue, raised by a Socialist father, consorting with Socialist friends like Eugene Debs, John Reed, Emma Goldman, the young Max Eastman. She simply decided, early on, to specialize in Sex. She propagandized for contraception on both feminist and social engineering grounds, even appealing to nativist sentiment with the argument that it was desirable to control the breeding habits of lesser breeds. Her defenders treat this as a brief aberration, and so it was: but it shows that much of the attraction of birth control (and abortion) lies in its potential for controlling other people's birthrates. The lesson has been taken to heart in Germany, China, India, and a number of Southern states.

Since Mrs. Sanger's triumph in the forum, people have increasingly thought of Sex as a pastime to which reproduction is incidental, and often inconvenient. Between our technology and her ideology, the whole meaning of physical love has changed for us.

The problem, obviously, is not contraception in itself, but the way it has habituated us to imagine ourselves and to reconceive our rights and obligations. This has created, or sharply accentuated, a conflict of interest between parent and child: a conflict easily resolved by redefining it as coincidence. For today, children are no necessary consequence of Sex. They are uninvited guests, party-crashers. Abortion therefore belongs to the logic of Sex, not of economics. Though abortion is often justified in terms of what people can afford, modern society can obviously support far more children than previous ages could. Today it is spoken of less as a misfortune than as an actual injustice that anyone should be afflicted with "unwanted pregnancy." And how presumptuous that anyone so afflicted should be "forced" to bear an "unwanted child" — meaning, to bear the natural and foreseeable consequences of a biological act. We now hear the grotesque argument that it's good for a child to be aborted if its mother doesn't want it, since nobody could want an unwanted existence. The same sort of conflict also exists between parent and parent: what if one parent wants a child (or an abortion) and the other opposes? Who decides, and how?

This much seems likely: the decision will not remain solely with the individual or the family. Under Socialism, neither is sacred; the family isn't indissoluble, or even special; and nothing will be inviolable if it opposes the state's purposes. And even under freer regimes, the state will step in when authority is unsettled. When marriages are dissolved, the state must assign the children to one parent or the other. That is inescapable as long as the public demands divorce. But the state now claims the power to declare unborn human beings subhuman. If it doesn't itself kill those it has so designated, it claims the right to delegate the killing.

What most people haven't yet noticed is how the state's interests may clash with those of the individual. So far the individual's freedom and discretion have been held to be total, arbitrary, not subject to rational scrutiny. But such a freedom immediately becomes vulnerable when the state brings its own rationale to bear. Already we have heard a few voices foretelling, and even advocating, mandatory birth control as a population policy. Personal preference won't count for much in a showdown with the armed and amplified modern state.

Neither the individual nor the family is a natural institution, in the sense of existing outside civil society. They are *creations* of civil society. I mean, of course, the individual and family endowed with legal status and rights. When civility breaks down, these things perish. The breakdown can be imposed from above, but it can also come about by popular demand, even in the name of "reform."

C.S. Lewis noted that many allegedly progressive doctrines of our time had the ultimate effect of eroding the human community and all its moral traditions, a process he summed up as "the abolition of man." He found in such doctrines the common error of supposing that man somehow "creates" his own values. In his scattered ruminations on this theme, one finds him tracing the heresy, apparently, to the Renaissance doctrine of sovereignty, known at first as the Divine Right of Kings, according to which the ruler's commands become the subject's obligations, *no matter what* — i.e., even if they contravene what would otherwise be common morality.

## Socialism
*In loco parentis*

A handy doctrine for warmongers, no doubt. But what interested Lewis wasn't the royal prerogative in itself. The deeper error was to think that Will could be the standard of Right — a question on which Lewis sided with Aquinas and Hooker in denying that even God's will could make right what was metaphysically wrong. Yet the heresy had survived its monarchic embodiment, and the Divine Right became democratized. Later theorists held that some sovereign will — that of the people, the *Volk*, the revolutionary vanguard — constituted the subject's obligation, even that the subject was doing no more than obeying himself. Under such doctrines, modern states pretended to redefine human obligations. Politics became the means of man's abolition. Old forms of authority fell. Education was replaced by conditioning — or, as it has lately been called, "re-education."

It is no accident, as the Socialists say, that Socialism and Sex (or "free love") came in together as "advanced" ideas. They supplement each other. Russian dissident Igor Shafarevich, in his profound book *The Socialist Phenomenon*, explains that the Socialist project of homogenizing society demands that the family be vitiated or destroyed. This can be accomplished in good measure by profaning conjugal love and breaking monogamy's link between Sex and loyalty. Hence, in their missionary phases Socialist movements often stress sexual "liberation," and members of radical organizations may impose mandatory promiscuity within the group, everyone sharing a bed with each of the others, each equally related to each. It is the ultimate in leveling.

Socialist regimes, once established, may appear puritanical. It is true that they forbid public erotic expressions; these are as tightly controlled as other forms of expression, which shouldn't surprise us. But the Socialist state has no need of a sexual campaign when it has already destroyed the essence of the family with easy divorce and abortion, surveillance, and the threat of sanctions against parents who teach their children religion. Christian children may be sent to orphanages, because children belong principally to Socialist society, and to instruct them in religion is to subvert the state by corrupting its members. The "accident" of biological relation gives a parent no claim on the child that can rival the state's.

The Socialist mind loathes what it calls "accidents" of birth, and applies this invidious term to every advantage a child receives. Pressed to the limit, this means that every benefit you give your own child amounts to a kind of deprivation for every other child. Unless parenthood has that privilege, unless family relations enjoy priority over the relations that obtain among citizens, Socialism must regard special favors as injustices. Hence the Socialist regime must be forever correcting and undoing the work of Nature, who is partial to her own. This is the rationale that lies beneath our "affirmative action" programs; they have less than they claim to do with race and history. Some extreme egalitarians even argue that physical beauty and native intelligence must be compensated for by "society," since they are undeserved. Socialism can't rest until the family is either abolished or reduced to the lowest administrative unit of the state. In Sweden it is now against the law to spank your own child (and even a good scolding may count as "child abuse"). The Socialist, it has been said, would aid the orphan by destroying the family.

In America Socialism doesn't sell under its own label, as I have said. But it is still real enough; the heresy is global. Most American liberals are more or less unconscious Socialists. There is no reason to shrink from so identifying them. Giraffes may be unconscious of being giraffes, but the zoologist goes by his own taxonomic purposes. Or, to use another image, the world Socialist phenomenon may be likened to a beehive (an image Shafarevich also finds useful), which consists of several kinds of bees — queen, workers, drones — all of which cooperate without comprehending the system they compose. Different though they are, they work in harmony to create a certain kind of order. Workers and drones don't (ordinarily) attack each other. Neither do liberals and Communists.

Most liberals are far less lucid than Communists about the ultimate shape of the order they are working to produce. Liberals' minds are much more *ad hoc*. But behind all their organizations — civil rights, feminist, civil libertarian, consumerist, environmentalist, sexual, homosexual — lurks a Socialist model. They want a certain kind of regime, almost always requiring a bigger and more centralized state power. They show the greatest reluctance to criticize the Socialist bloc and they attack, ridicule, and wax hysterical about those who do. They are not only alert to benign signals from that bloc, they fall for all its dissimulations, but they maintain hostile suspicions toward anti-Socialist forces. They insist there are no values worth fighting over separating us from the Socialist powers, with whom they desire "normalized" relations, but they prescribe severe sanctions against Chile and South Africa. Willmoore Kendall, reviewing a book by Chester Bowles about the "developing" nations, noted with amusement that Bowles had at bottom a simplistic view of the whole melange of Muslims, Buddhists, Hindus, cannibals, nomads, aborigines, herdsmen: all their "aspirations" seemed to be Socialist! Clearly Bowles illustrated the psychological phenomenon we call projection. Thus does the Socialist mind homogenize the most diverse realities. Too *many* evenings? It is hard to see how any spirited or intelligent person can bear Socialism for *one* evening.

Under the guise of personal freedom, the leftist hive has gutted many of the institutions through which freedom is mediated. The hive defined the family as a repressive institution, and mounted assaults, in the names of sexual liberation and civil liberties, against all the local and traditional supports of family structure and authority. Two of our most oligarchic and centralizing forces — the Supreme Court and the mass media — have done the dirty work which representative institutions could hardly have done: the Court has mandated "change," the media have advertised and marketed it. The first great step was to force the cutting back of local censorship. The second was to legalize abortion. All this was justified as constitutional imperative that warranted bypassing the usual legal and political processes, and celebrated as the "opening up" of American moral life. In reality it meant Socialism, a central power immune to popular resistance.

Few Americans will buy a bottle labeled Socialism. The cunning of the Socialist hive has consisted largely in its skill in piggybacking on more attractive things. Like Sex.

# A Nation of Loners

*September 1, 1989*

*Love and hope and peace and mud — that was Woodstock, apotheosis of the counterculture. The Dionysian energies released there were supposed to transform the nation, and, alas, some of them did.*

In early 1969 a quartet of young promoters decided to stage a weekend rock festival in Woodstock, New York, two hours from the Big Apple. At first they figured on 25,000 fans. But as they lined up 27 acts for the August date, the projection grew. They were prepared — in food, sanitation, and medical facilities — for 150,000 people.

That turned out to be about a third of the total. Tickets were selling for $6 a head, but every hippie in the Northeast had heard about the big party, and by Friday, August 15, the roads to Woodstock were clogged with old Volkswagens crammed with scraggly-haired kids intent on three days of sex, drugs, and rock.

The promoters had rented a field from a dairy farmer named Max Yasgur, and hoped to keep freeloaders out with makeshift fences. No use. The entire hippie economy was based on freeloading, and the minimal security arrangements couldn't cope with a half-million unexpected guests.

The townspeople had been nervous about the invasion. In fact, the festival wasn't allowed in Woodstock itself — it had had to be relocated to Bethel, fifty miles away. In those days upstate people were still afraid of hippies, especially in groups of 500,000 or so.

By Friday night the excitement was tremendous. None of the *really* big stars of rock — the Beatles, the Stones, Dylan — were there, but the roster was still impressive: Jimi Hendrix, Janis Joplin, Creedence Clearwater Revival, The Who, Johnny Winter, The Grateful Dead, Jefferson Airplane, Blood, Sweat, and Tears, Joan Baez, Arlo Guthrie, and such newcomers as Joe Cocker and Crosby, Stills, Nash, and Young. Later, having been at Woodstock would become a mark of status, for performers and fans alike. This was to be a legendary weekend.

Hippie events tended to be — well, unstructured. To give you some idea of *how* unstructured Woodstock was, Abbie Hoffman was partially responsible for security. Additional security was provided by a former standup comic named Wavy Gravy (*né* Hugh Romney), who ran a commune out west called the Hog Farm. A slight hitch developed when the Hog Farmers threatened to leave in protest against the killing of mosquitoes. The promoters had had the field sprayed with insecticide. For some hippies, insecticide was right next door to genocide.

Woodstock finally got under way, though not without a few more hitches. For one thing, it rained. Hard. Since shelter consisted almost exclusively of sleeping bags, this caught the crowd off guard. But they were having too much fun — ecstasy, really — to mind very much.

The rain didn't help the music, either. Acoustic conditions were already less than Van Cliburn might have wished: loudspeakers blaring into a pasture, rendering even Jimi Hendrix inaudible to much of the throng.

The festival was attended by federal narcotics agents, who did make a hundred arrests for sale and possession of hard drugs, but made the strategic decision, lacking a half-million jail cells, to let pot-smoking ride. Marijuana enjoyed de facto legalization for the nonce. As for sex, there was plenty of it. In the general camaraderie, total strangers shared soggy sleeping bags. By day, some of them simply shared exposed patches of ground. Toplessness and nude bathing (in nearby ponds) were frequent.

It was all very Dionysian, a mass rejection of the false values of Ozzie and Harriet. From the bandstand, Country Joe McDonald led a joyous chant: "Give me an F! Give me a U!" until the crowd had spelled the *whole word,* bellowing it out in unison, not caring a whit if Nixon and Agnew and J. Edgar Hoover heard it all.

Leftist politics was taken for granted, but only as a sort of backdrop. When Abbie Hoffman tried to hog the microphone to deliver a political message while The Who was performing, Pete Townshend belted him from behind, decking him. Abbie scrambled off the bandstand and didn't come back.

Apart from that incident, all was peace and nonviolence. A gentle hippie oversoul seemed to suffuse the festival. As Wavy Gravy put it, years later, "The universe took over and did a little dance.... And you could just feel these little tendrils of invisible energies kind of like — I felt at times like a marionette almost." Strangers had become brothers and sisters, smiling beatifically at each other with chemically induced inner peace.

But by Saturday afternoon, there were more hitches. The field was sheer mud. Food had just about run out. So had toilet paper. The Port-O-Sans smelled so foul that people were using the earth itself, and it was getting ... noticeable. One youth was run over in his sleeping bag by a tractor hauling away Port-O-San deposits; he died.

At one point there was a serious scare. Several helicopters were approaching ominously. Was Nixon launching an aerial assault? No. It turned out that the U.S. Army and National Guard were flying food and medical supplies to Woodstock Nation. On Sunday morning more food — eggs, doughnuts, cereal, milk, sandwiches — arrived, courtesy of local residents. Woodstock Nation had quickly become reliant on the adult world it had tried to do without for the weekend. About the only thing there was no shortage of was drugs.

Max Yasgur's farm, green on Friday, was a brown expanse of mud, garbage, and hippie dung when everyone left Monday morning. The odor lingered strongly for nearly a year. Even after that, for two more years, you could still smell it every time the weather was hot — the afterbirth of a nation.

Woodstock is a legend now. If you weren't there, you are given to understand, you really missed something — an unrepeatable instant of hope and joy and brotherhood, and an epiphany of a better world that might be. "It confirmed my sense that class, race, and gender divisions could be transcended," one participant is quoted as saying in *Life*'s twentieth-anniversary commemoration of the magic weekend. Many others speak in the same tones. There has been talk of recreating the moment, but the idea has been tied up in legal wrangles over promotional rights.

Pundits can't seem to resist talking about Woodstock in grandiose terms. Shortly after the event, *Time* spoke of it as auguring a new value system that could change (for the better, of course) the American national character. Today, it is generally lauded as a milestone of the counterculture.

Which it was, in a way. *Life*'s delirious quotations from celebrants are more than balanced by others who speak of the drug abuse, their own subsequent problems with drugs, the friends who later died from overdoses. Several of the rockers who performed at Woodstock have also died, most of them from drug excesses. Abbie Hoffman, who resurfaced after ten years on the lam for a cocaine rap, killed himself in April, using sleeping pills.

Another glory of Woodstock, free love, has also come a cropper in the years since. Like drugs, it has been a source of personal and social devastation over time. The cult of the ecstatic moment looks much less promising than it did in 1969. The destruction has been worst in the chief target of liberal solicitude, the black inner cities. Dionysus has worn out his welcome.

Even so, nostalgic books and articles on Woodstock flood us. Most of them suggest that the weekend utopia in the mud stands as a model for emulation.

But despite the grand terms in which Woodstock is praised (and sometimes denounced), one of the laudatory books, Jack Curry's *Woodstock: The Summer of Our Lives* (just published by Weidenfeld & Nicolson, $19.95), inadvertently touches on what may be the real meaning of the event: "This had been a convention of 500,000 people who had always thought they were freaks, alone."

Janis Joplin said something like that to the crowd from the Woodstock bandstand: "We used to think of ourselves as little clumps of weirdos. But now we're a whole new minority group." A year later she was dead, of a drug overdose. (She was also alcoholic.)

*Life* quotes another Woodstockian: "I flung myself into the counterculture without looking back. It seemed like the outcasts had found acceptance. I had friends for the first time."

Woodstock enabled such people, multiplied by a few hundred thousand, to think they were the wave of the future, their leaning on each other an event of world-historical importance. But to read Curry's book is to find, between the lines of congratulation, a series of sad case histories of kids who had always felt like losers, until the big party. And afterward. There is the pathos of self-delusion in the way they profess to have drawn sustaining — almost salvific — inspiration from an inordinately publicized rock concert.

Woodstock's mythic status as a peak spiritual, cultural, or political moment is belied by the way these poor kids couldn't even manage a mildly rebellious weekend without succor from grown-ups. In a way, one could wish it had at least been a case of flaming youth burning off animal energies. It was so much less than that. Even its devil-may-care image is too flattering.

Doesn't anyone remember the Sixties? The hippies weren't rebels. They were positively hungry for authority. They settled for the only form they could get, which was peer pressure. Their "rebellion" was all fashion and imitation, mass-market bohemianism. The long hair, love beads, and tie-dyed jeans were the nearest approximation to a uniform they could achieve. They all talked alike, in a studied slang that adults, on casual contact, found refreshing and exotic. It got dull very quickly. The stereotypes were true because hippies mimicked each other. They were usually lonely and unloved kids who felt they had to be each other's role models. They were wrongly suspected of wanting to destroy society when they were only destroying themselves. As at Woodstock.

Loners have a way of finding each other. What Woodstock proves is that when their numbers reach critical mass, they become a market, and you can herd them together and tell them things they desperately want to hear from somebody: that they're winners, that they constitute a nation, that they hold the hope of the world, and that all their unresolved personal problems are really only one big political problem that can be solved instantaneously. Some of them will go on believing it for twenty years.

# Howard Beach:
# The Use and Abuse of Race

*March 27, 1987*

*Warning: The following article contains material that some will consider "bigoted." Parental discretion is advised.*

On the Friday night before Christmas, a gang of young toughs in Queens, New York, beat up three men who'd been hanging around a local pizzeria. One of the three, trying to escape, was hit by a car and killed.

Later that night, the gang, or one just like it, beat up an off-duty fireman it caught taking a break outdoors. If it was the same gang, they needn't have bothered. They could have taken the rest of the night off after the first attack, and rested on their laurels.

Not being literati, they didn't realize they'd already created the literary event of the season.

The second attack was barely noticed. But the first put Howard Beach on the map, and captured the imagination, such as it is, of the nation.

The first three victims were black. The attackers (and the fireman) were white.

And that was the story: a "racially motivated" attack that left one black man dead. Even if you counted it as a murder — as the special prosecutor eventually did — it was only one of about twenty thousand across the country last year. But it set off a verbal riot in the media — a terrifying wave of editorials, follow-ups, opinion columns, Op-Ed pieces, sermons, analyses, synecdoches, metaphors, diagnoses, prognoses, predictions, and imprecations.

The cancer of racism! Just beneath the surface! Howard Beach is only a symptom! Alarming increase of racial incidents! Nationwide pattern! Disturbing similarities! The first step is to acknowledge it! Climate that encourages discrimination! Policies of the Reagan Administration! Signals that racism is again "respectable"!

Civil-rights leaders and demonstrators poured into the streets, accompanied by legions of reporters and TV cameras. Governor

Cuomo took the local DA off the case and named a special prosecutor. One of the blacks and his lawyer charged a coverup and refused to cooperate. Mayor Koch called the crime "a racial lynching" and "the most horrendous crime" in all his years as mayor, spoke at a Howard Beach church (where he was shouted down), popped up on the Op-Ed page of the *New York Times,* and called for a federal commission to study the problem, the *cancer,* of racism.

And the pundits: Jack Newfield, Roger Wilkins, William Raspberry, Carl Rowan, William Buckley, Murray Kempton, Jimmy Breslin, Norman Podhoretz, Don Feder, Ray Kerrison, yours truly, and many others all had a say. *Time* and *Newsweek* and the TV networks gave it big coverage. The New York press stayed on the case, day after day, stepping over the corpses of victims of subsequent murders while following the Howard Beach story.

Details emerged — about the kids (one had dated a black girl, who spoke warmly of him), the victims (one stabbed his girlfriend a few days after the crime, when she woke him up too early), the neighborhood (the people were afraid of crime and resented being made a symbol of racism). The rhetorical tide swelled and sank, and swelled again: First Howard Beach was a lowdown blue-collar Italian sort of place, a hotbed of the Wrong Attitudes; then it became more Understandable, no worse than the rest of the country, and so forth.

The *Times* editorial page droned on: "… racism is once again on the rise … ugly incidents on half a dozen campuses … Reagan Administration … civil rights has receded from the national consciousness … Americans must be willing to confront …." *The Village Voice* did a major spread: "… senseless attack … raw hatred and fear … New York has been loathe *[sic]* to confront its own racism … deeply ingrained … first step is to bring it out in the open and acknowledge it …."

*The New Republic,* however, walked off with the prize for ritual incantations, leaving all the other Foes of Bigotry gasping far behind. A single editorial contained (I've skipped the ellipses) "view each other across a gulf of physical and psychological separation mutual suspicion and ingrained hostility shameful stains on American society that must be eliminated insensitive to the concerns of blacks worst residual instincts among whites our flawed democracy dangerously counterproductive remaining economic and social barriers to the full and equal participation of black people in American life the cycle of poverty dependency and underachievement that now defines the lives of more and more black people the historical experience of racial oppression elimination of racial discrimination continuing necessity to experiment with new solutions outdated fears the role of government is to provide the kind of moral leadership enormous waste of human potential" The miracle of word processing!

The winner in the Precious Conceit category was Jack Beatty, writing on the *Times* Op-Ed page. He managed to tie Howard Beach to the territorial instinct, Reagan's deficit, and Immanuel Kant. Sample: "President Reagan's deficit, indeed, institutionalizes irrationality." Creative writing, indeed. Roger Wilkins, same page, saw Howard Beach as part of a Pattern, which included Klan rallies, Reagan policies, and books arguing that the welfare system doesn't work. Charles Murray's *Losing Ground* led to Howard Beach.

Bill Buckley tried to restore perspective by pointing out that a country whose favorite TV program is *The Cosby Show* can hardly be called "racist." I'd go further. Cosby appeals to white America's nostalgic affection for an endangered species — the Vanishing Negro. He's what we *thought* we were going to get by passing civil-rights laws, and what we wish to hell we'd gotten.

## II.

What actually did happen at Howard Beach? Nothing much, in the sense usually understood. Was it a "racist incident"? Maybe, maybe not. If you're out with your buddies looking for trouble on a Friday night, and you find three colored guys from another neighborhood, they'll do. And if you club them with baseball bats, what are you going to call them — "Afro-American citizens"? No, you'll reach for the obvious epithet. You'll *make* it a racist incident. If you find a white object for your attentions, you'll have to come up with something else.

In a country of a quarter of a billion people, it would be surprising if there weren't an explicitly white-on-black crime now and then. If the whole country is "racist," there should be quite a few of them, and any single one shouldn't rate national attention.

So why did Howard Beach get so much media coverage? An indirect answer comes from Thomas Friedman, Jerusalem bureau chief of the *New York Times,* grappling with the question why Israel, a faraway country the size of New Jersey, gets so much media attention. The answer is *not* the number of Jews in the American media, he argues, since the European press gives Israel just about the same amount of coverage. The answer is that Israel has mythic resonance for all Westerners.

"Men have never taken the world just as it comes," he observes. "We need to explain the world to ourselves, and, to do so, we have used stories — myths and fables — to record our experiences and shape our values. In most cultures, these narratives are tied together by what has been called a 'super story.' Religions are a super story. Ideologies can be a super story. The super stories determine which information about ourselves is important and which is not. Where Israel comes in is that it is central to what is simply the oldest, most familiar super story of Western civilization. The Bible is the first edition."

He quotes Yaron Ezrahi, an Israeli political theorist: "The Bible, the original super story, still constitutes the controlling myth of Western civilization, history, and religions. No other story, no other vocabulary, no other framework of understanding can match its familiarity."

All news is "biased," in that it's the selection of information in accordance with tacit standards of relevance. We notice the bias when the news is chosen to fit a "super story" the audience doesn't necessarily subscribe to. All earthquake stories are biased against earthquakes, but the bias is unanimous, and nobody complains. But the super story behind the Howard Beach story was Racist America. The very fact that it was empirically atypical made it all the more dramatic as a synecdoche.

The reasoning is spectacularly circular. To validate its original heavy coverage, the *Washington Post* sent a reporter to talk to the residents of Howard Beach, some of whom obligingly talked about "niggers" and otherwise spoke in an idiom nice editorial writers don't employ. One said: "I hate black people and I always will. I'm prejudiced and I'm proud of it." Others referred to the local integrated high school as "a jungle." The *Post* had the story it was after — just as it did when Janet Cooke wrote her Pulitzer Prize-winning story about "Jimmy," the eight-year-old black heroin addict, with the minor difference that Miss Cooke invented her facts. The moral was the point, and the moral remained intact.

"News" consists not only of high-impact events, but of local events of low impact that can be assimilated to pet myths. But most journalists are unaware of their commitment to myths, and think of themselves as, in Dan Rather's words, "honest brokers of information." You don't shoot the messenger for bringing bad news! Except that the messenger exercises a lot of discretion as to which news to deliver. If the mailman did that, he'd lose his job.

As long as they get their chosen facts straight and deliver the news and the cues in deadpan fashion, journalists tend to think they've satisfied the canons of "objectivity." Keep overt moralizing out, keep "fact" segregated from "opinion," and you've done your job. Because they usually do this, journalists can't understand why conservatives see them as liberal. They are, of course, but they're sure it doesn't show, at least not very much.

And conservatives haven't always specified their complaints very well. "Accuracy" in the media isn't the primary problem; there are keen professional scruples about accuracy, and you can't blame people too much for occasional honest mistakes.

The real problem resides at a higher level of abstraction. The media are so saturated with myth that it's fair to see "news" as an early stage on the assembly line whose final product is a *New York Times* editorial. The Howard Beach incident, of no national importance in itself, offered an occasion to attitudinize. It had less to do with raw "fact" than with *l'art pour l'art*. It achieved the maximum ratio, this side of Janet Cooke, of opinion to datum.

That's why I call it the literary event of the season. It was, for properly cued *Times* readers, what the death of Liberace was for readers of the *National Enquirer*.

Miss Cooke fouled out. She violated the minimal condition of the game by making up the central peg of Fact. But the facts she made up demonstrated her grasp of the game itself. Black, poor, child, neglected, heroin, ghetto, illegitimate: She was perfectly keyed to sentimental fashion. She chose the correct symbols, and her publisher commended her for "telling it the way it is, rather than the way it's supposed to be."

Her version is still essentially "the way it is," and her lack of Fact to validate it means only that she had ventured, ahead of her time, into *pure journalism*. The public wasn't quite ready for it. A stubborn convention insists that the journalist adhere to representational canons — which are not, after all, very demanding — and forbids the great leap forward from the prevailing Impressionism to Abstract Expressionism. But it's coming, it's coming. The logic of the art requires it.

**III.**

Take a typical *Times* story: "Papandreou Devalues Drachma," or something along those lines. It's news, of sorts: It happened on one day, rather than another. But it poses no menace to the *Times*' sober secular *Weltanschauung,* the way, say, a UFO story or an account of a miracle at Lourdes would. At that level, most "news" isn't new: It's the self-confirmation of a closed perceptual field, from which major deviations are automatically screened out.

The perceptual field is constituted by myth: a "super story" imbedded in certain metaphysical assumptions. History has such-and-such a form: Watch — we'll show you how the day's events illustrate it. Emphasis is accordingly given to those events which prove the *Times* editorial page was right all along. Disconfirming evidence has to sneak in, at the tail end of a story on page 27, unless of course a specific story on South Africa, "social" spending, the Pentagon, "civil rights," disarmament talks, Chile, abortion, and various other perennial topics. It also limits criticism of the Soviet Union: Since socialism is never criticized *in principle,* negative attention attaches only to details like the treatment of "dissidents." This costs little, since the Catholic Church's internal discipline is likewise covered as a matter of persecution. As for Communist persecution of Christians, it hardly registers: Christians, especially Catholics, are reactionary, and, according to the mythology, progressives *can't* persecute reactionaries. It doesn't make sense! So Jonestown was treated not as a story of a left-wing fanatic ("Let's die like good socialists, friends!" Jones said, ladling out the Kool-Aid), but as an object lesson on "cults," religious zealots.

The mythology also generates an etiquette, a set of progressive proprieties, breach of which can mean embarrassment and even political ruin. The most famous example was James Watt's crack about having appointed "a black, a woman, two Jews, and a cripple." Ed Meese caught hell for saying there was little real hunger in America, when everyone *knows* there's "invisible poverty." The media carefully observe the progressive etiquette, beginning with diction: "black," "gay," "spokesperson." One of liberalism's great coups has been to transmute ideology into etiquette: A code of behavior in minutiae is awkward to argue with. The wrong opinion, the wrong word, can be a headline-making "gaffe," a social blunder, disclosing lack of compassion, unraised consciousness, "insensitivity." Note that "insensitivity," or offending progressive sensibilities, is a vice — whereas "irreverence," offending reactionary sensibilities, is a healthy, spunky, refreshing sort of thing.

Zeroing in on reactionary "gaffes" is a media genre in itself: the embarrassing close-up shot. It's done to Jim Watt, it's done to Howard Beach. The selective attention is that of a roving searchlight, looking for culprits to embarrass, rather than the neutral relaying of "information."

Aware of their power and at least half aware of their predilections, the media have coined a pair of self-justifying phrases to incorporate their denial of ideological animus: "investigative journalism" and "the adversary press." These at least suggest that there's *initiative* behind the patterns of media attention, although they are meant to be accepted as assurances of tough-minded, politically impartial skepticism. Media skepticism is selective, though. Lyndon Johnson didn't meet the "adversary press" when he was pushing the (progressive) Great Society programs: He ran into it when he pursued the (reactionary) war in Vietnam. Richard Nixon got adversary treatment all along — except when he took the (progressive) step of reaching accords with Communist rulers. The correct phrase for what we're talking about is Embarrassment Journalism, and what the media want to embarrass is the Right. It's a reflex. They can hardly imagine any alternative. Their entire nervous system is progressive.

That's why the news seems so profoundly repetitive. The media are forever seeking evidence to vindicate their own prejudices. And every prejudice can find such evidence. As soon as the Iran-Contra business was dubbed "-gate," the sorts of data that would be reported were clear: The case was assigned to the same super story as Watergate.

The TV camera was made to order for the cheap synecdoche, the quick news bite that can be presented as a symbol, an iceberg tip. The media prated about "the sleaze factor" for months, then made a big story of a pair of cufflinks Meese had been given. Howard Beach was victimized by just such camera tricks. Every bit of ethnic slang uttered within earshot of a reporter was suddenly eligible for massive amplification. *Newsweek* quoted a bit of racial graffiti it found at Smith College. National news is anything that gets reproduced nationwide. Half a dozen graffiti, collected from divers parts, constitute a "nationwide pattern."

**IV.**

And "racism." What's that?

It used to mean something definable: a belief in the superiority of one race.

Is Howard Beach racist? Is America? The first point to observe is that the word now has no definition and would lose most of its utility if it did. It's a piece of liberal billingsgate, a name without a thing, though liberal social philosophers discuss it as if it were a real substance, like Pythagoreans discussing the quintessence.

The second point to observe is that it's not up to anyone to decide whether he himself is "racist." It's not a matter of squaring things with meanings any more. We're in ideological Wonderland now. If the relevant opinion cartel declares you "racist," you're racist.

So what those questions mean is this: Are Howard Beach and America the kinds of things that the people who declare things "racist" would declare "racist"? And the answer is obvious: Yes.

Think of all the energy expended nowadays *avoiding* being declared "racist" (or "sexist," or "homophobic"). The charges emanate from amorphous clouds of attitude, and amount to cues to others of like attitude to look, note, smear, ostracize, boycott, denounce, deplore, or bomb, as time and means afford. An informal defamation league takes care of these matters.

Little provocations suffice. Subtle turns of phrase have gotten the aforementioned Buckley declared "racist" on several occasions. (After all, racism *is* subtle.) It works on the barking-dog principle: One barks, they all bark. Only the first knows why. Bishop Berkeley (no pun intended) had it right: To be is to be perceived. If you're "perceived" as a racist, you *are* one, until the perception wears off.

The *Washington Post* reports that residents of a certain part of Queens have become diffident about saying where they live. "Nowadays, when we are asked where we are from, we say New York," one said. "Howard Beach has become infamous." The media have created a brand-new prejudice, against Howard Beach. So its people now hope to "pass" — that's what it's come to. The world has learned to associate Howard Beach with one thing.

But isn't that only natural? It's what we all do: We go on the information we have, plus mental associations. That's why people make rapid judgments about race, too.

What do you associate "black" with? Africa? Slave ships? Lincoln? Jackie Robinson? *Brown* vs. *Board of Education*? Martin Luther King? Or the kid who took your wallet? Say the latter, and you can be ... declared. All the others are conventional literary associations; they're safe. Bring it down to personal experience, especially of the unpleasant kind, and you're asking for trouble from the opinion cartel. You run afoul of the dominant taboos, the progressive etiquette.

Certain things may be known and acted on, even by *Times* editorial writers, but they mustn't be said, unless you're sure the progressive thought police aren't around. Never mind the First Amendment, pal. That's for pornographers and Commies.

You're in the subway, and there's a kid sitting nearby. Nervous? That depends. Without saying a word, he "gives off" information about himself, voluntarily or not. One of the data is his race. That counts — along with height, weight, dress, demeanor, eye movements, and a lot of other things you don't note discretely. You react, while trying not to seem to be reacting to *him,* for reasons of prudence, shame, courtesy. You edge away, maybe. You won't tell anyone about this. No reason you should. It may happen several times a day, and you forget it quickly each time. You're glad you don't have to explain it all to some goddamn sociologist, who might regard *you* as the guilty party. And maybe you are. But you've got to be careful.

So much enters into these little encounters, so much more than you can tabulate: observations, intuitions, memories, associations, rumors, judgments, to the sum of which John Henry Newman gave the fancy name "the illative sense." That's how the mind works when the mouth is shut. Newman summed it up succinctly: Everybody has a reason, but not everybody can *give* a reason. It would be fanatical to treat race as the only factor, but it's doctrinaire to demand that it not be *one* factor. We're not supposed to notice it? Ah ... the color-blind society. Remember? The forces of Social Progress used to talk about that, but even they couldn't make it work, so they came up with affirmative action: Race may be noticed, but only for progressive purposes. You can even make invidious racial generalizations, provided they're about whites, Howard Beach, America. You can say what a violent society this is, so long as you don't narrow it down to who's committing so much of the violence.

Sometimes all you have to go on are stereotypes, broad impressions. They are no substitute for more refined knowledge, but they may be a stepping stone to it. "All stereotypes are more or less accurate," says John Murray Cuddihy, a sociologist. Sociology, after all, is among other things the study of distinctive forms of group behavior. It can say in Latin things we're forbidden by the taboos to say in plain English. A "bigot" can be defined as a guy who gets caught practicing sociology without a license.

So I'm saying racial prejudice is okay? Please. I'm not an idiot. One of the problems with trying to discuss ethnic matters in good old First Amendment free-speech let-it-all-hang-out Age of Candor America is that the minute you depart from the ritual cant, you have to prove you're *not* saying so many things. The ideology of the taboo-mongers posits bigotry everywhere ... just beneath the surface ... in all the lacunae of idiomatic speech, more or less the way the old physics posited the ether filling all the unexplored space of the universe. They think it *must* be there, so for them it's always plausible to impute it. "Civil rights" is now based on the presumption of guilt — against whites. If you're not in lockstep with Progressive Attitudes, you're a bigot until proven otherwise.

Not that there aren't a lot of bigots in this society. That's why I'd like to kill those little bastards in Howard Beach who gave all white people a bad name.

# Writing on the Wall

*September 4, 1981*

Two decades ago the Berlin Wall went up nearly overnight, the most brutally unequivocal symbol of the division between our flawed civilization and the clumsy barbarism that threatens it. In August the occasion was commemorated by two major American publications.

*Life* did itself proud, with an astonishing 17 full pages of color photos of the 4,500-mile border of the Socialist Bloc, at every point of which soldiers stand ready to kill those who flee. If there is any political fact in this world from which it should be possible to take your moral bearings, this is it. The armed border most vividly exemplified by the Wall means that the hundreds of millions of people within are quite simply slaves, property of the states that confine them. If you haven't seen *Life*'s pictures yet, do. Meanwhile, I can't do better than to quote Jed Horne's accompanying text:

"It's not the first time a great power has tried to secure the margins of empire behind bulwarks of metal and stone. But the Iron Curtain is in one fundamental sense unprecedented. The Great Wall of China, Hadrian's Wall built by the Romans across the north of England — every other fortification of comparable scale has been a barricade thrown up against the threat of invasion. Unique in history, the Iron Curtain is predicated on the need to keep subject peoples penned in. After a few early modifications and continued remodeling over the years, it has become a remarkably effective prison."

With calm eloquence and perfect historical and moral perspective, Horne has said, in a paragraph, the essential truth about a subject the major media have contrived to evade ever since the mid-Sixties. It is almost startling to encounter such sanity in a popular magazine. Like many painful topics, the real mechanics of Communist oppression have been surrounded by taboo and euphemism.

Consider the way the same anniversary was handled in the *Washington Post*. In its Sunday Outlook section, the *Post* chose to turn the subject over to a veteran correspondent named Dick Rosse, who simply sneered the whole thing away. In a long, rambling memoir of his own Berlin experiences at the time, Rosse stepped around the central issue as if it had been a land mine, scoffing instead at American officials who spoke of (in his phrase) "U.S. determination, etc."

Rosse recalled with special affection Alfred Hitchcock, who, at a press conference, made light of the Wall — a bit of "irreverence" Rosse found "refreshing," in contrast to the "solemnity" with which our diplomats and politicians treated the whole business.

"Actually," he wrote, "all of us newspeople profited from the wall. Both in terms of money and career advancement." Many people turned the Wall into "a merchandisable commodity." "Our daily lives changed little during the crisis … There was plenty of boozing and sleeping around …." After a general account of the merry cynicism that prevailed, Rosse more or less concluded that this had been the right attitude: "Those of us who were there on Potsdamer Strasse in August of 1961 will not lift a glass to join in East Berlin's celebration. But we might retire quietly for a solitary glass of wine and recall some memories that weren't all that unpleasant."

Not that Rosse was wholly cynical. About our side, yes. But not about the other side. He explained, for the benefit of those who might have missed Walter Ulbricht's pronouncements at the time, that "the rationale for the wall was entirely defensive." Irony here, you think? Not at all. "East Germany was hemorrhaging," you see. The refugees included "irreplaceable" engineers, doctors, workers, and farmers whom "the East Germans" — not, mind you, the Communist regime, but "the East Germans" — "desperately needed." The "press lord" Axel Springer — not the *publisher* Axel Springer — urged people to defect, while "more responsible voices" urged them "to stay on the farm and the hospital and the classrooms."

We have been endlessly reminded that with the death of the *Washington Star*, which ceased publication the weekend Rosse's article appeared, the capital of the Free World has become a one-newspaper town. This became a cliché so fast that I didn't give it much thought.

But it is sobering that the Free World's capital's single newspaper — one of the two or three leading newspapers in the nation, the one most of our federal officials read every morning — sees fit to mark the anniversary of the Berlin Wall with a flippant *defense* of the Wall. Rosse and the *Post* are no doubt entitled to attitudinize lightly about American officialdom. But to turn this sort of urbaner-than-thou "irreverence" toward official rhetoric into a total derogation of the freedom of East Germans, penned inside a huge political prison — that's different. That's serious — no matter how bantering the tone, how glancing the apology for the men who keep the prison.

In fact it would be a big improvement if the Rosses of the Free World had the gumption to defend the Wall as honestly as Jed Horne attacks it. But how could they? The essence of their decadence lies in their preference for evasion and innuendo. Such are our "more responsible voices."

# Piety For The Future

review of
*Christian Humanism: A Critique of the Secular City and Its Ideology*
(Franciscan Herald Press 1979) by Thomas Molnar

*April 27, 1979*

Secular humanism (as Irving Kristol has pointed out) is virtually an established religion, with the added advantage (as James Hitchcock has pointed out) that it doesn't suffer the disabilities currently imposed on acknowledged religions.

At one time it was plausible to say that this humanism was common sense, plus a little science and history: reason herself as she speaks when liberated from superstition and dogma. It was the light at the end of the tunnel of the Christian era, when man would return to the sunny rationality of the ancients, a condition enhanced by modern scientific method. This view is expressed in the very names given to historical eras: Dark Ages, Renaissance, Enlightenment.

Specialists in these areas have long since found that such terms fit only very loosely, at best. A new historiography, exemplified in the work of Eric Voegelin, has suggested a radically new scheme, in which humanism is found to be, not mere secularism, but a positive creed, an ideology, informed by the Christian heresy of Gnosticism, and even traceable to that heresy as promulgated in the twelfth century by Joachim of Flora.

Joachim predicted the advent of a new "Age of the Spirit," in which man would outgrow the need for Christian and ecclesiastical authority and achieve an autonomous perfection. Although modern humanism adopts profane accents, its structure remains that of the old heresy, so it is not strange that secular humanism should find allies within the church from which the heresy sprang in the first place. Hence the phenomenon of Christian humanism, which cooperates with the superficially secular brand in seeking to impose utopian regimes. The superficiality of the differences is apparent in that formal credal positions seldom inhibit that cooperation. The distinction between a George McGovern and a Robert Drinan seems merely sartorial.

In *Christian Humanism,* Thomas Molnar sketches the shape and history of that ideology. He wisely reminds us that many of the ancients were offended by Christianity in the first place because of the very "humanism" of the Incarnation: what an indignity for a god to become a mortal! It was like becoming a head of lettuce. Given this apparent derogation of divine transcendence, it was inevitable that humanistic excess should become a permanently tempting position for Christians.

Molnar finds adumbrations not only in Joachim but in more familiar figures like Nicholas of Cusa, William of Ockham, and Pico della Mirandola. Contrary to modern mythology, the Renaissance's optimism about human potential was not a return to paganism, whose fatalism (cf. Homer, Aeschylus, Aristotle, Vergil, Seneca) gave little warrant for faith in human perfection or general progress. Ancient man saw himself as locked into the natural order. Pico saw man as "fashioner of his own being," or as Molnar puts it, "a pure indeterminacy": a phrase that places Pico nearer to Sartre than to Sophocles. *Christian Humanism* abounds in such startling linkages; among other things it is an excellent short genealogy of a nihilism that was conceived in hope. Sartre's Nothingness didn't come out of nowhere. In defining man as the desire to be God he is in a sense deeply traditional.

The doctrine of the Incarnation makes the transcendent God paradoxically present. The paradox is intellectually unfathomable and psychologically hard to bear; the easy way out is for man to seek to "abolish this duality and turn, single-mindedly, toward tasks that his earthly existence prescribes to him."

Yet the idea of divinity, once known, is less easy to banish. It becomes assimilated to humanity entirely. Man becomes God, in a reversal of the Incarnation. When the conception of man is collectivized, the entire human race becomes the locus of divinity. Man is the measure of all things, but this "man" includes men unborn. Since it is obvious even to ideologues that those men who now exist are far from perfection, divinized man must be something as yet unrealized, a "new man," man as he will (according to ideology anyway) be.

Thus humanism gives its energies to utopian politics. Having abandoned the eternal, it loses interest in (and even resents) traditional criteria of sin and virtue; personal behavior is a matter of concern only as it bears on man's collective destiny. (Exit chastity.) The real action is at the level of the state. Those who think that what has happened to American government can be summed up as "secularization," as in abortion, have failed to notice the way secular humanism (backed by the Christian kind) has aggressively tried to engulf traditional values.

Profound and incisive as usual, Molnar identifies the project of Christian humanism's theology: "the complete assimilation of the Church to the World." But that world is the world of the future — as imagined by humanism itself. And if we are to be "open" to the future, as the Rahners and the Kungs tell us to be, how, Molnar asks, can they presume to say in advance what it will be like? If they already know its nature, they hardly need wait and see.

The secret of humanism turns out to be not that it is open to the future but that it is closed to the past and therefore to the permanency embodied in the past. It is really a posture of revolt and repudiation, its idealism an excuse for demolishing the actual. And its deepest sin is ingratitude.

# Unbelievers

*March 7, 1980*

If there were a Thomas Aquinas among us, his talents would be needed to supply irrefutable proofs of the Soviet Union's existence. A great many people seem unable to believe it's really there.

The unbelievers, in fact, tend to dominate the mass media — or did, before Afghanistan. A man who had spent the last decade glued to his TV set would never have supposed the Soviets were engaged in an enormous military build-up, still less that any use would be found for all those weapons.

But the media need drama, which means conflict, which means villains. In the selection of villains the operative principle has been James Burnham's Iron Law of the liberal sensibility: the preferred enemy is always to the right. Long after it had ceased to be possible to idealize the Soviets, it remained impossible to have a Soviet villain in a movie or TV show. So we have had a spate of Nazis (and neo-Nazis), multi-national corporations, mean Southern sheriffs, and other subjects of editorial deplorings. If *I Led Three Lives* were a TV series today, Herb Philbrick would have to be depicted as a threat to civil liberties.

One doesn't have to be particularly of the Right to sense that something is missing. The idea that Nazis holing up in the Amazon jungle could still pose a threat to anyone suggests an obsession that overwhelms all sense of actuarial reality, but you're more likely to see a film based on that assumption than on the obvious fact that, say, the KGB kills people.

It's one thing to celebrate the Allied victory over the Nazis and Fascists. It's something else to suggest that the immediate peril is from octogenarians who have made a breakthrough in genetic engineering, as in *The Boys From Brazil*. Imagine a movie about Sioux Indians preparing to scalp the citizens of Bismarck, North Dakota, in 1980.

On a recent Sunday morning I happened to be watching the Catholic program *Insight*, which I had never seen before. Sponsored by the Paulist Fathers, it raised the question, How would Christ be treated if he came back today? It tried to answer this question with a parable.

In what appeared to be a Latin-American country, a group of street clowns tries to amuse and edify the people. Their leader is named Bobo (Martin Sheen). Just then, a new regime takes over and starts arresting people, including the clown troupe. What for? For suspicion of subversion. The generalissimo orders Bobo brought to him. He explains his position — that the nation needs law and order, and protection from the Marxists — while offering Bobo a share in the rich repast his servants are bringing in, and promising more benefits if the clowns co-operate with the new order.

Bobo, who until then has seemed as frivolous as Mork from Ork, suddenly reveals himself as a shrewd liberal (if you can accept the concept). He bats down the generalissimo's excuses for tyranny, pointing out that the nation's wealth belongs to the people — an unprecedented idea that causes His Excellency almost to swallow his cigar. No compromise is possible.

Bobo is taken out to face a firing squad. He keeps clowning merrily to the end, confounding his thuggish captors. From their prison cell, the other clowns watch him die, and sing a song of ultimate triumph, in which they are joined by an American tourist in the cell, whose consciousness has been raised by his own false arrest. Clearly the new fascist regime is doomed.

Get it? Bobo is Christ. There is no point in belaboring a minor and sappy piece of work for a vice it shares with so many other things. But the persecution of Christ *does* go on today, and if we're talking about either scale or intensity we have to look first at the Communist world. If anyone should be singled out for ignoring what nearly everyone ignores, it should be Christians who affect to enlighten us while concealing what James Hitchcock has identified as the Dirty Little Secret of liberal Catholics: the perduring Communist war on religion.

One needn't be a cold-warrior to notice this. It's perfectly possible to be a pacifist or an isolationist or even a common liberal, and to think all military conflict with the Soviet Union should be avoided, while taking note of the actuality of Communist life — not blueprint "Marxism," but Communism as she is lived. In fact, people who stand morally neutral between the two super-powers, without patriotic or strategic commitments, are in the best position to make the purely humanitarian case against Communism. Why are they afraid to?

The media are saturated with trendiness, and in a way this includes even those cheap, pitiful little Sunday morning productions in which some religious order tries to prove its relevance by simulating prime-time metaphysics. Today's bold prophets — the real ones — are the people the Western media ignore. They are the Christians behind the Iron Curtain, and the Free World Christians who smuggle Bibles to them.

You won't see these people on television, but you can get a most moving glimpse of them in a little book called *The Persecutor*, by Sergei Kourdakov (published by the Fleming H. Revell Company, in Old Tappan, N.J.; $1.95). Kourdakov used to kill Christians; then, revolted by his life, he fled the Soviet Union and became a Christian himself, trying to warn the West against the evils he had helped perpetrate. He was only 21 years old when despair or the KGB caught up with him, just outside Los Angeles, in 1973.

# Rainbow in Central Park

*July 9, 1982*

The worldwide community of socialists, overt, closet, and latent — the Hive, as I like to call it for short — has invested heavily in the peace movement, and the June 12 nuclear freeze rally in New York, coming so soon after major demonstrations in Europe, was bound to be a major event. The Hive had to go for broke.

An enormous amount of planning went into the June 12 rally. Several avenues in Manhattan were barricaded off and supplied with extra police, at a cost of more than $1.25 million, not to mention the losses to merchants. The city freely imposed these costs on taxpayer and merchant alike. After all, who could object? Who wants to die in a nuclear holocaust? Mayor Ed Koch went along with the pretense that the occasion was as uncontroversial as that.

The newspapers carried detailed maps showing where various categories of marchers should gather: children, religious groups, the disabled and elderly, educators, labor unions, performing artists, women's organizations, gays and lesbians, computer technicians, and — oh yes — "political organizations." This last implied that all the others were apolitical. That was significant, as it turned out.

Around the country hundreds of buses were lined up. Parking areas awaited them at points as remote as Yankee Stadium, Kennedy Airport, and Hoboken.

As a rule the Hive prefers a euphemistic language in America, where overt socialism is unpopular. But times are changing: this was the next thing to a coming-out-of-the-closet party. The national sponsors of the June 12 rally included the Communist Party U.S.A. as well as Americans for Democratic Action (the Hive's right wing, as it were).

The organizers announced their purposes: "To support the United Nations Special Session on Disarmament and to call for a freeze and reduction of all nuclear weapons and a transfer of military budgets to human needs." Human needs? Uh-oh. Sure enough, Ronald Reagan was attacked by name, and his budget cuts were said to "hurt black, other minorities, and women" *[sic]*. Of all the world's governments, "the U.S Government is the least willing to stop its nuclear insanity."

All this was right up front, yet it got curiously little attention in the media, which preferred to notice only the platitudinous. The Hive itself was tactically divided about how explicit to be.

A revealing little scene occurred on the *Today* show the morning before the rally. Orson Welles, who was to be master of ceremonies at the climactic gathering in Central Park, tried unctuously to head off the suspicion that the whole thing was some sort of left-wing do: the freeze movement cut across "all classes and ideologies," he said. "You'll find people from the whole spectrum."

With Welles was Randall Forsberg, mother of the freeze movement, but much less the accomplished media smoothie. At first she played along with Welles, saying that the proclaimed message of the rally was "simply that the United States and the Soviet Union should stop the nuclear arms race."

But then Jane Pauley mentioned the name of Ronald Reagan, triggering unsuspected atavistic furies: Forsberg immediately launched into a protracted squawk about Reagan's attempts to "deflect" the movement.

Welles acted swiftly, deftly. Patting Forsberg on the wrist, he said he really had to disagree with her, and (giving it an extra squirt of unction), "Let us give Mr. Reagan the benefit of the doubt."

Nice going, Orson. This was national TV — no time for angry buzzing. A lot of those folks out there had *voted* for Reagan, and there was no percentage in showing them all which way this swarm was heading. Let's just talk about something we can all agree on, shall we ... save the stinger for Central Park ... for now the note is, Who knows, maybe even President Reagan — and he *is* our President, even if we disagree with him — maybe even *he* will see the light, once he sees how people of *all ideologies* feel about the prospect of nuclear war ... we don't want Ma and Pa Heartland out there to get the feeling the Martians are coming!

**Lining Up**

Saturday morning was gorgeous. Sunny, clear, not too warm. IT'S HOLMES, blared large stacks of tabloids, but nobody in town seemed to care about last night's heavyweight Armageddon. They had the Main Event on their minds.

Kids from Texas were gathering on the side streets feeding into First Avenue, carrying placards and wearing cardboard hats shaped like nuclear warheads. They had a cheery, non-ideological freshness about them. They seemed excited to be in the Big Apple. You got the impression they hadn't read the organizers' statements too closely.

On 51st Street the (overt) political organizations were waiting, all of them hard leftist. The Communist Party, for instance. The Socialist Labor Party. The Communist Workers' Party. The Young Workers Liberation League. Committee in Solidarity with the People of El Salvador. People's Antiwar Mobilization. The Marxist-Leninist Party, U.S.A. League for the Revolutionary Party. U.S. Anti-Imperialist League. (I didn't see any sign of the National Committee to Reopen the Rosenberg Case, though it was listed as one of the rally's sponsors.)

Bullhorns on stationary trucks blasted out invectives against Reaganism and U.S. imperialism. Lapel buttons demanded U.S. withdrawal from El Salvador. Leaflets and newspapers seemed almost to drown out the bullhorns: "To Fight Nuclear Weapons, Fight Imperialism!" "Step Up the Fight Against the U.S. Imperialist Warmongers!" "National Call to Form a Coalition Opposed to the Reagan Administration." "Nuclear War in Lebanon?" "No More Excuses — U.S. Disarm Now!" "'Peace' Under Capitalism Means World War III." "Socialist Revolution Is the Only Alternative!" "Join the June 14 Nonviolent Disarmament Blockades." "Disarm the Pentagon." "Freeze: Reagan's Pro-War, Anti-People, Racist, Sexist, Anti-Lesbian/Gay Program!" "Will Reagan Legalize Assassination in the U.S.?"

Yet most of the marchers (about 150,000, by later estimates) avoided these extremes. They stuck to mild, banal slogans ("Choose Life"), though some were mildly witty ("Save the Earth: A Good Planet Is Hard to Find"). A remarkable number were from Vermont, where a nuclear freeze has been endorsed at 177 town meetings — including a town called Orwell. What did it mean to the Orwellians that there were a few Communists around? Why should they exhibit a provincial intolerance? ("Good grief," said one annoyed Vermonter, "does everybody in New York think we're just a bunch of country dummies?") This demonstration was *pluralistic,* after all — open to *all* ideologies. As the *New York Times* would later put it, this was a "rainbow spectrum" of political organizations. "It's hard to label this crowd," Abbie Hoffman told a *Washington Post* reporter.

It was colorful, for sure. Placards. Effigies. Masks. Floats. Balloons. Banners. Costumes. Huge puppets. Guys dancing on stilts, admirably nimble. A huge inflatable rubber whale labeled "Save the Humans."

Tom Wolfe was there, looking over the artists' and writers' contingents. Most of them were unrecognizable: *soidisants*, probably, from art schools and writing courses, except for Arthur Miller. An interviewer approached Wolfe and asked if he was in sympathy with the march. Not really, he said. He saw no sign of any awareness that the great threat to peace might just be coming from the Soviet Union. He couldn't recall a single instance of two democracies going to war against each other.

Nobody seemed to know, in fact, that the Soviet Union was just then fighting a war in Afghanistan. Nobody seemed to be reminded by this march of the Popular Front days. Here was the largest demonstration in American history to proceed under the partial auspices of the Communist Party, but nobody wanted to make a big deal of that. Instead we heard the insistent theme that all this somehow transcended politics: it was the *aperçu du jour*.

The march began near the United Nations, turned up 42nd Street, met another body of marchers at Seventh Avenue, and turned toward Central Park. Signs announced delegations from the Vermont towns, from Utica, Montreal, Tibet, Japan, Iran, Palestine. Placards and banners denounced the United States, Israel, China, Khomeini. In the ecumenical spirit of the day there were Catholics, Episcopalians, Presbyterians, Baptists, Unitarians. The ecumenical spirit probably accounted for the absence of "cold-war rhetoric" (Hive-talk for criticism of the Soviet Union).

In the afternoon Central Park was absolutely jammed. The marchers had been joined by 400,000 or so others (some estimates put the total number of people upwards of three-quarters of a million). Last September, a half-million had come just to see Simon and Garfunkel. This time the entertainment was supplied by Jackson Browne, Linda Ronstadt, James Taylor, Peter, Paul, and Mary, and — naturally — Pete Seeger. The entertainment was free, but there were the interminable commercials: speeches by Robert Drinan, Bella Abzug, Helen Caldicott, Coretta Scott King, William Sloane

Coffin, Elizabeth Holtzman, Barry Commoner. Speakers, need one point out, representing all ideologies.

The organizers' statement had made plain the dual object of the rally: "disarmament and social justice ... the disarmament and social justice movement ... social justice and peace ... an end to the nuclear arms race and a shift in resources to improve the nation's economy, create more jobs, and meet human needs ... peace and new priorities."

This was also the dual agenda of the speakers, who, from their many ideological perspectives, attacked Ronald Reagan (Liz Holtzman also got in a kick at Richard Nixon, for old times' sake) and blamed the arms race for the suffering of poor people, blacks, women, the Third World, and babies everywhere.

A libertarian of the anarchist persuasion might have suggested dismantling not only the Pentagon but also the whole range of social programs threatened by Reagan. Would the speakers have accepted this deal, if it would avert nuclear war? Sacrifice even socialism for peace? To ask the question is to realize at once their real agenda. But of course such questions did not come up in this rainbow spectrum of ideologies. There were no libertarians in sight; no supply-siders for a freeze; no Jehovah's Witnesses; no neo-Nazis for whom the menace of universal destruction took urgent priority over even the imperatives of racial purity. And of course Reaganites (a mere 50 per cent of the voters) were excluded in advance from this monochromatic rainbow. For that matter, considering that this was New York, there were remarkably few Jewish groups. (I saw none, myself, though *The Village Voice* mentioned something called Jewish Dykes for Life.)

All ideologies, eh, Orson?

## They Don't Sting Each Other

That night the local TV newscasts showed clips of the event. Some camera crews had gotten interviews with celebrities in the park audience. Roy Scheider, the actor, said something about how awful nuclear war would be. Jill Clayburgh said, "This isn't politics — this is *life!*" Anchorpersons kept using the same phrase: "broad coalition."

Little of the anti-Reagan rhetoric came through, except an occasional exasperated suggestion that the problem was that Reagan doesn't seem to appreciate what nuclear war would *mean*.

The TV reports kept stressing that the march and the rally at the park had been peaceful. There was an odd undertone of relief, even gratitude. Imagine: a peaceful peace demonstration! There was something almost paradoxical about it. Clearly "peace" has taken on strange connotations — which is what usually happens when the Hive appropriates a word.

But why *shouldn't* it have been peaceful? Welles had suggested that the various groups were forgetting their differences for the nonce, as if it were ordinarily an explosive social risk to invite liberals and Communists to the same party, except when the very survival of humanity was at stake. Come off it, Orson. Bees from the same hive have a certain diversity of function, but they don't sting each other.

### 750,000 Can't Be Wrong

The next day the good grey *New York Times* actually waxed lyrical. It devoted a front-page story and two full pages within to the rally. Seven stories in all, with headlines like "A Spectrum of Humanity Represented at the Rally."

"A kaleidoscope of humanity — young people and old, rich and poor, the famous, the forgotten, and countless thousands in between.... They represented a rainbow spectrum of religions, ethnic groups, trades, professions, unions, cultural and educational institutions, [and of course] political organizations ... diverse gathering ... There were poets, actors, corporate executives, transit workers, teachers, students, housewives, doctors, store clerks," etc.

A student was quoted: "Demonstrations are usually a political issue — pro-Communist, pro-socialist. But this is pro-existence." And a policeman: "This march is for everybody." A *Times* reporter, under her own by-line, exulted along with them: "And they were every kind of person, there for many reasons.... There were demonstrations in the past that were implicitly exclusionary.... But yesterday there were parents and children, whites and blacks, veterans and conscientious objectors, Montana Cowboys against Nuclear War and the Puerto Rican Socialist Party, Grey Panthers and a punk contingent with Mohawk hair tinted fuchsia."

The lead editorial reasoned judiciously: "Hundreds of thousands of demonstrators in New York's Central Park can't be wrong."

## Whose Kaleidoscope?

For this occasion the *Times* abandoned its usual demeanor of critical skepticism. It went even further. Not only did it not *criticize* the stated purposes of the rally: it didn't even *state* the stated purposes of the rally. Not one of its seven stories — totaling over eight thousand words — found room for the thirty words in which the organizers had spelled it out. Instead the *Times* took pains to imply that the event was essentially apolitical and that the attacks on Reagan (glancingly mentioned in one of the seven stories) were somehow incidental. Needless to add, the *Times* evinced not the slightest discomfiture that so many people should gather under semi-totalitarian auspices. (A rally under the auspices of everyone from the Libertarian Party to the National Socialist White People's Party, though more truly diverse than this one, would probably not have qualified as a "kaleidoscope of humanity.")

The rally was actually a broad coalition of people who hate the West and people who don't hate people who hate the West. It was, rather frankly, leftist. Yet the *Times* felt it had to protect the demonstration from itself, for the sake of the great cause of progressivism — just as Welles, the veteran media wizard, had felt compelled to prevent Forsberg from blowing the whole thing on national television.

The *Times* knows that the progressive cause advances fastest, in the long run, when it proceeds under the cover of conservative forms. The coded euphemism is all-important. And so, on the following Tuesday, a brief *Times* editorial scolded New York's openly leftist Channel 13 for covering the rally with "reporting that at times was strident and loaded." The reporters had said "Wonderful!" whenever a speaker assailed Reagan. They "sounded like cheerleaders" and "abandon[ed] professional standards," grumbled the *Times*. Such tactics "pollute public confidence."

Careful, children. You're scaring Ma and Pa Heartland! And we want them to come to the next rally! Why be so strident about it, when the Hive has such a rich vocabulary of soothing buzzwords?

**Buzzwords**

**coalition.** Any alliance of implicitly socialist groups.

**cold-war rhetoric.** Blaming the Soviet Union for international tensions.

**humanity.** Man as conceived by socialism. All **humanity** is presumed to be at least latently socialist.

**human needs.** Socialist or redistributive programs.

**ideology.** Non-socialist point of view. The Hive, however, presents itself as comprising many **ideologies**.

**imperialism.** International influence opposed to socialism.

**labels.** Clear identification. People in the Hive like to say they **reject labels**.

**liberation.** Release from constraints of non-socialist traditions.

**peace.** Enfeeblement of non-socialist powers.

**political.** Overt. Openly socialist groups are **political organizations**.

**priorities.** Subordination of anti-socialist to pro-socialist tendencies.

**progressive.** Favorable to, or tending toward, socialism.

**social justice.** Control of national wealth by a socialist regime.

**strident.** Tactlessly candid about real issues at stake. Overt socialism invites **labeling** by the enemy. On the other side, **cold-war rhetoric** is always **strident**.

# Mavericks in Lockstep

*October 14, 1988*

The American Civil Liberties Union has become a minor issue in this year's presidential campaign, thanks to Michael Dukakis's "card-carrying" membership in it. But while George Bush is taking heat for alleged anti-Jewish activities by people in his campaign — activities he knew nothing about — Michael Dukakis is not being held accountable for the public positions of an organization he is (well, used to be) proud to subscribe to.

The notion that the ACLU is some sort of "watchdog" over the Bill of Rights is wrong. Its interpretation of the Constitution is selective, shaped by a political agenda.

To take a couple of obvious examples: the ACLU interprets freedom of the press to mean that the sale of porn magazines and movies involving kids, even babies, is constitutionally protected under the First Amendment. This is known as "expanding our First Amendment freedoms." How nice. But is the ACLU interested in expanding our Second Amendment freedoms too? You know, the right to keep and bear arms? Not at all. The ACLU actively supports gun-control legislation.

The ACLU takes a liberal political line whose predictability is only occasionally broken by its willingness to move a little ahead of the herd, as on kiddie porn. On many issues — abortion, gay rights, racial busing and quotas, crime, school prayer — it insists that the Constitution not only permits a liberal agenda but in some cases, actually mandates it and permits nothing else.

Now this is a peculiarly rigid way of reading the Constitution, which ACLU types usually like to praise as a "living document" whose interpretation requires openness and flexibility. Some critics stress the ACLU's left-liberal agenda; William Donohue's book *The Politics* of *the American Civil Liberties Union* documents and analyzes this very well. But my own dislike of the ACLU has a different source.

The ACLU is an outfit for mediocrities who like to think of themselves as mavericks. A real maverick won't join an organization with an orthodoxy about political issues over which disagreement is natural and consensus rare. He won't kid himself that all his political preferences (and those of his friends) dovetail nicely with the Constitution. He knows that life is more problematic than that. He realizes that there are tensions between desire and convenience, between what he says he always wants and what he actually wants on Tuesday. The real maverick doesn't try to paper over these ironies; he savors them, even in himself.

Once upon a time there was a genuine maverick, H.L. Mencken by name. As it happens, Mencken had a run-in with the ACLU in 1938 over the clash between its professions of principle and its real agenda. Its national board was loaded with Communists and fellow-travelers who argued that the violation of civil liberties in the Soviet Union should be excused because the goals of Communism were so noble.

"If the bosses of Russia are free to abolish civil liberties in order to attain some chosen political end," Mencken wrote, "then the bosses of the United States are free to suspend them in order to attain some other end." He took wry note of the "interlocking directorates" of the ACLU and the American Communist Party.

Things haven't changed too much. The leftist lawyer William Kunstler, a member of the ACLU's National Advisory Council, has said: "I do not believe in public attacks on socialist countries where violations of human rights may occur."

The ACLU celebrates "pluralism" and "diversity," but its own positions are dismally monochromatic. Yes, it really is a wonderful thing to expose your mind to various views, so that you can carry on a sort of internal conversation among them. But the mark of the pseudo-maverick is that even though he reflexively defends bizarre forms of dissent, his own mind is never shaded and subtilized by carrying variety within. Instead, it assumes the sort of crude momentum some people mistake for logic, which reasons that in order to protect *Ulysses,* you have to protect kiddie porn too.

If you want the country to move leftward, and if you think the best strategy for achieving that is to use the courts rather than the elective/legislative process, then the American Civil Liberties Union is the group for you. But please, don't try to tell me your card-carrying membership signifies your dedication to independent thought.

# No-Fault Media Bias

*January 25, 1980*

*Political liberty is good only so far as it produces private liberty. Now, sir, there is the liberty of the press, which you know is a constant topick. Suppose you and I and two hundred more were restrained from printing our thoughts? What then? What proportion would that restraint upon us bear to the private happiness of the nation?*

Thus Dr. Johnson, in a typically querulous *jeu* of blasphemy against this or that little idol of modernity. Idol? Yes: in its vaunting, nothing-is-sacred irreverence, the press worships only itself. Liberty of the press, a/k/a the First Amendment (never mind the part about religion), remains a constant topick today, because the press remains the arbiter and custodian of constant topicks.

The late seventeenth century produced a naïve but persisting ideal of the citizen as reader. On the view detectable in writers as diverse as Milton and Locke, man is naturally, almost helplessly independent-minded. Persecuting men for their opinions is not only wicked: it's silly. They can't help what they think. Rational man became identified with literate man. Milton and Locke both wrote optimistic little treatises on education. (Johnson thought both injurious.)

With a book in his hand, man could recover his pre-lapsarian solitude, could reflect undistracted on the experience distilled in print and then re-enter society for a profitable exchange of views with his fellow reader-citizens. The intellectual's utopia is a nation of bookworms. The publishing industry has always cottoned to this picture. It is still the ideology of the publishing class. Educators like it too. That is why we subsidize literacy on such an enormous scale. And so uncritically. It is boorish to ask, What good is it? People assume (conveniently) that you don't want a serious answer. You must be anti-intellectual.

Johnson loved books but didn't worship them. He sensed what was going on: print is a form of mass-production, and not the least of its effects is to standardize opinion. If it makes intellectual independence possible, it also makes intellectual conformity probable. There is no necessary connection between literacy and logic. The alphabet as such is a mere code, just like the Morse code, mastery of which is a very minor mental achievement. And in fact (as the volume of junk mail attests) its only indubitable value is that it creates new forms of manipulation. Lenin was only the first modern totalitarian to want a totally literate populace, to facilitate the centralization of power. Yet foolish Westerners are always mightily impressed by the "eradication" of illiteracy. They hardly mind, or notice, that with this can come the virtual elimination of personal privacy.

Any correlation between liberty and literacy is hard to specify. That, I take it, was Johnson's point. He saw that books (more especially periodicals) promote cant, and cant is a mechanical substitute for thought. Reading removes us from the realm of direct experience where we can exercise personal judgment. Literate company invites us to talk about things we are essentially ignorant of. Almost inevitably we tend in such a situation to utter the received opinion. It's safe. Many writers have noticed that "public opinion" itself is a kind of artifact, the result of having a large body of print-consumers in search of intellectual hearings. Historian John Lukacs distinguishes between "public opinion" and "popular sentiment": the first is part of the decorum of a culture dominated by print; the second, more spontaneous and disreputable. Uttering bits of "public opinion" establishes one's communion with respectability, whereas uttering "popular sentiment" shows one's vulgarity. The good reader-citizen tries to transcend the gross element of popular sentiment around him by echoing the loftier sentiments he has gathered from the refined company of books and their periodical extensions.

The irony of course is that what is supposed to pass for independent opinion is itself imitative. Literacy descends to farce in *cliché*. Hugh Kenner treats this theme with hilarious insight in *The Stoic Comedians*: he sees Swift and Flaubert as playing with the artifices of print, satirizing the conventional views print has purveyed. *A Modest Proposal* and *Madame Bovary* can be read as mockery of the abstracted reader who, like Don Quixote, has finally lost touch with actuality. And Edmund Burke sneered at English radicalism as the fiction of a "literary cabal" who tried to hide their "total want of consequence" with "noise, and bustle, and puffing, and mutual quotation of each other." One of the main polemical strategies of *National Review* has always been to emphasize the high ratio of sheer silly convention in liberalism and radicalism.

The electronic media exploit the enormous prestige of the printed word by presenting themselves as extensions of the book, entitled to all the privileges and immunities of press freedom. But this misconceives their real nature, which fosters not detachment but the sensory immediacy from which books deliver us. At the same time, we misconceive books by supposing them to be mere extensions of speech, when they are a completely different thing.

The usual and understandable assumption is that freedom of speech came first, and then, on the same principle, freedom of the press. After all, speech is natural, and the press is a gadget. But as Leonard Levy has shown, it really happened the other way around. Press freedom came first. The power of the press eventually won its independence from state controls. Once that was established, and only then, freedom of expression trickled down, so to speak, to the individual speaker. Has there ever been freedom of speech where the press wasn't free?

It is impossible to compute the value of a free press. True, civilization can do without it — as long as there is no press at all. But the reason the press, once it exists, must be basically free isn't that the press is a good thing, but that it's a dangerous thing. Just because it creates a community of opinion it must never fall into the hands of the state entirely. The more you deplore it, in fact, the more ardently you must want to keep it separate from the reigning political power. Everything it does wrong it does worse when it becomes the organ of officialdom.

Besides, *pace* Dr. Johnson, every freedom is probably ill-used by most who possess it. But as Friedrich von Hayek shows in *The Constitution of Liberty,* each freedom must be presumed precious for the sake of the tiny minority who make use of it, in the long run, to the benefit of all. The real value of press freedom may have little to do with the cocky pretensions of its vulgar apologists.

We do a lot of arguing about those pretensions without having a very clear idea of what the mass media are and do. Liberals and conservatives alike tend to accept the myth that the essential business of the media is to inform. Liberals think they do this well, on the whole. Conservatives think it is fairly easy to do it well, but that the media don't, because the people who operate the media allow their political biases to shape the presentation of otherwise neutral facts. I think both views are naïve.

Personally, I don't object to what the mass media do half as much as I object to what they think they do. And I also object to conservatives' notions of what the media ought to do. All of which requires some explaining.

We conservatives grind our teeth when Walter Cronkite tells us "That's the way it is" and when the *New York Times* claims to deliver "All the news that's fit to print." But we assume — don't we? — that these claims are false largely because of the human failures of those who make them; assume, moreover, that these human failures are essentially avoidable, and that the claims *might* be true, if only the media people would be more self-critical and purge their reportage of political biases.

I think we have it backwards. It would be truer to say that if the media folk were more self-critical they wouldn't make their claims in the first place, and that their political biases are the result, not the cause, of the bogus claims. It is simply impossible to give a daily play-by-play of history that is both objective and comprehensive. In fact it is impossible to be *either* objective *or* comprehensive. If it were so easy to be definitive, there would be no need of scoops, and muckraking, and leaks, and investigative journalism, and the like; all of which imply that truth in its wholeness is terribly elusive. And imply, moreover, that we get just such fragments of truth as certain strategically placed people are disposed to seek, pursue, notice, or reveal.

The very necessities of selection and emphasis rule out objectivity. News implies human interest of some kind, not mere random information: news is drama. The illusion of objectivity is the cultivated result of the reportorial suppression of affect. A good reporter doesn't tell us, or even let us guess, which side he personally takes. But some sort of bias is built into news if only because it is addressed to a specific, if broad, audience. If reportage appears disinterested, that is because news people try, skillfully, to appeal to a *consensus* of interest without seeming to favor *particular* interests.

But this works only up to a point, because part of what divides the audience is precisely which stories ought to be placed on the agenda of public attention. I agree that most network news reflects, on the whole, a certain liberal bias. But part of the explanation is that the very convention of reporting news as fully, accurately, and disinterestedly as possible is a Western convention. And to do this on a global scale you need a worldwide acceptance of the legitimacy of this convention. When no such acceptance prevails, the result is a kind of automatic and built-in bias that favors anti-Western regimes. Which brings us to the central problem.

Usually we think of the decline of the West in material, military, and economic terms. But the decline is also cultural. Much of the world is in revolt against Western spiritual and intellectual values. The rulers of the Third World don't regard gathering information as an innocent activity; at the United Nations they persist in offering resolutions affirming the sovereign right of a nation (read: any regime in power) to control "the flow of information." At home they are increasingly adopting the quaint custom of harassing, threatening, expelling, excluding, and in some cases killing Western reporters.

This is and has long been especially true in the "socialist" countries, where truth is a national resource, as it were, and reportage severed from commitment to the national purpose is inherently subversive ("counter-revolutionary"). Nowadays this view is catching on fast. The socialist camp is expanding, and even in non-socialist Iran Khomeini has threatened to throw out those foreign reporters whose version of the truth offends his version of Islam. Those who remain are there at his sufferance, and in the current crisis they have been useful to him, or they might have been expelled before now.

To the shock of many newsmen, "objectivity" is proving no guarantee that they will be exempted from the hostility that has attached to other Westerners. What is shaping up is a world in which the media have less and less direct access to facts. The turmoil may have at least the healthy effect of reminding us of what was so easy to forget while things were relatively static, say from 1945 to 1975: that the news we get is contingent on political circumstance. We have been hugely scandalized by little ad-hoc government coverups in the West; we have barely noticed the standing policies of virtually total coverup in Communist countries.

When the news media affect to give us a total picture of the world, they naturally neglect to remind us that we are seeing only what they have been able to discover. It would be pretty monotonous for Cronkite to repeat every evening that, of course, we don't really know much of what's going on in the Soviet bloc. And besides, it would be deflating to the orotundity of "That's the way it is" if he had to keep qualifying it with admissions of that sort: the news would seem so disturbingly partial and tentative, so little in command of truth, so much at the mercy of circumstances beyond our control. It would lose its oracular authority.

What makes the problem worse is that the news industry tends more and more to the pictorial. Led by television, even the news magazines are now stressing sensory immediacy (color photography) at the expense of verbal reportage and analysis. The whole form of news subtly de-emphasizes the things that can't be shown directly and drains them of reality. We forget or discount what we can't see on TV. The worst media bias is in a sense imposed by totalitarian regimes that force the news media to stay home, keeping our attention on domestic problems. The free press of the West is only fully free *in* the West. So far, unfortunately, it hasn't made this as clear as it should. But the era when it could keep downplaying or ignoring this may be coming to an end.

For over a century the ascendancy of the West has allowed us to be un-self-conscious about our communications. The astute English cultural critic Raymond Williams argues that most of us tend wrongly to demote communications from its central place in human life: we "assume as a matter of course that there is, first, reality, and then, second, communication about it. We degrade art and learning by supposing that they are always second-hand activities: that there is life, and then afterwards there are these accounts of it.... [In reality] the struggle to learn, to describe, to understand, to educate, is a central and necessary part of our humanity. This struggle is not begun, at second hand, after reality has occurred. It is, in itself, a major way in which reality is continually formed and changed. What we call society is not only a network of political and economic arrangements, but also a process of learning and communication."

So in a way the barbarians are right: they understand better than we seem to that our communications system isn't neutral in its actual commitments and effects. They may describe it crudely as "imperialist," but they have a point: our media are a major constituent of our power.

Neither the Left nor the Right seems to grasp much of what this implies. Both assume that reporting the news is only incidental to American national interests. (Just as the Carter Administration assumes that international law is so sturdily autonomous that it will govern even if Western power evaporates.) The fact is that a community is virtually coterminous with its communications system. It is a very bad sign indeed that so many countries are now so totally seceding from civilization as to abolish the convention of respecting the emissaries and newsmen who keep us in touch with them.

What this may entail was recently illustrated when NBC cut a deal to interview a hostage in Teheran. The network agreed to broadcast the interview in prime time and to accompany it with a statement from a Khomeini supporter. "And now, a word from our sponsor." *New York Times* TV critic John J. O'Connor defended NBC against charges of unpatriotism on grounds that "journalism is not obligated to make the job of government easier." That is true as far as it goes. But it forgets that in accepting terms dictated by another government, NBC to some extent compromised journalism, making itself the tool of a regime in exchange for the privilege of access.

Journalism? What new information was unearthed? It's all very well to say we should tell the truth and let the chips fall where they may, but when we see journalists swapping prime time for carefully selected bits of the truth we are beholding an activity less exalted than the devoted pursuit of verity. Sensation has its value, but sensation isn't truth. TV journalism has more in common with TV entertainment than with print journalism.

If print is a form of mass production, TV is something even further from the paradigm of reflective citizenship. The term "mass communication" is a misnomer: communication means give and take, talking and listening, utterance and response. The essence of TV is to multiply and amplify sensation on a tremendous scale. The viewer can neither retain his detachment (as he can with print) nor reply in kind. Communication? Hardly.

The business of the mass media, whatever good intentions may modify it, is to attract and stimulate mass reaction. This makes them natural tools of totalitarianism, which has only come into its own with the electronic age. Even in free countries they are increasingly given over to advertising and pornography: forms of manipulation which, whatever their moral value, shouldn't be confused with the habits of reflection we associate with reading. And as I have said, reading itself is overrated.

The more sophisticated the mass media become, the further they take us from the ideal of differentiated individualism. This is why all the world's despots are eager to monopolize them. As the image replaces the word in popular consciousness, the common denominator of public opinion is lowered, intelligence becomes irrelevant, and the populace is reduced to something more and more like a sheer mass.

TV imagery itself is subject to a selection process it is hard to criticize to any effect, and the obvious danger now is that various governments will master the art of using our media, feeding them self-serving images much as our own politicians have fed them leaks, press releases, and other tendentious data. In order to cope with this we must free ourselves from old stereotypes about the ways the individual knows and the news accumulates.

Lately I've been spending some time at the CBS building on West 57th Street in Manhattan. It feels odd. To begin with, it's sealed off from its immediate physical environment, a rather seedy West Side neighborhood of delicatessens and car washes, the sidewalks abounding in winos and black plastic garbage bags. All within a few yards of Walter Cronkite. You wonder wryly what the First Amendment has to do with this locale.

First-Amendment-talk is full of the imagery of openness: the media giving us new vistas, broadened sensory access to the world. Maybe in a way this requires CBS to cut itself off, sensorily, from the rest of West 57th, an unreliable sampling of the world. Still, it's strange. You walk in off the dingy street and, like Dorothy entering the Emerald City of Oz, wait for admittance past the security guards. Then suddenly you are in a magically different place: streamlined, windowless, a buzzing concrete hive of engineers and electronic gadgetry which will beam a synthetic edition of Reality into the American home, with a Wizard's voice booming: "That's the way it is."

Hayek reminds us that in order to defend the free market's real value, we have to avoid making false and irrelevant claims for it, such as that the market rewards people according to their moral deserts. It is time the mass media quit pretending to tell us all about everything, and admit that they give us no more or less than an interesting and valuable sampling of certain of the day's events. If they acquire some modesty about their mission, they will be less tempted, in the tough years ahead, to support false claims by allowing themselves to be put to sinister uses.

# Acute Philophilia

*July 25, 1980*

The nation is in the grip of rampant Philophilia — the unnatural love of Phil Donahue. Liking him is one thing; how can you not like Irish charm, even after filtered through a generation or two of Americans? But *loving* him: waiting months for tickets to his show, shrieking at his entrance, hanging on his words: that's something else again.

Phil's thing is a quality you see especially in talk-show hosts. They call it honesty; I'd call it earnesty. Earnesty is when they're dealing with a heavy subject, usually sexual, and they lean closer to the guest and furrow their brows and lower their voice to an oleaginous stage whisper and ask the Big *(this is it)* Question: "Do you *really think*, Dr. Weltanschauung, that *this society,* with all its *taboos* and *hangups*, is *ready* to accept transvestites as *human beings* just like the *rest* of us?"

Phil is deeply into earnesty, and can relate to nearly anyone at a very heavy level. Imagine Ted Baxter with a social conscience, and you've got the idea: a lot of trendy talk-topics, a lot of words like voting and caring and supportive and concern, all emitted from the depths of a consuming vanity that is almost unconscious and therefore innocent. Phil's constituency is forty million housewives plus Ashley Montagu (who calls him "a public service, the best thing U.S. television has ever had. My wife and I watch him every day because we learn from him"). He flatters their intelligence, but puts them down bluntly when, during the studio-audience question period, they try, shyly, to take untrendy positions ("Do you think, just because you disapprove of what they do, homosexuals should be denied their *rights*?")

The technique, a mixture of romper-room condescension and abrupt sarcasm, reminds me of a professor I had in the Sixties, who never tired of cooing that we were the brightest generation in history. Things went smoothly as long as we agreed with him: all smiles and nods. But lo the poor fool who uttered a reactionary thought: suddenly the hapless student was made to feel like a piece of detritus left over from one of the less-bright generations. The professor's head froze in mid-nod, he glared silently, then (if he thought meet) delivered a cutting remark. The incidence of reactionary utterances fell off considerably over the semester.

Which was my way of discovering that the widely advertised intellectual training is only half the story of a modern college education. The other part is a subtle initiation into a set of trans-disciplinary liberal attitudes, effectively enforced by little more than the tacit threat of minor public humiliations. For most people, that's enough.

Phil Donahue isn't a liberal professor; in fact he went to Notre Dame back when it seems to have been a stronghold of orthodoxy; and there, as he tells us in his autobiography, *Donahue*, he was a dutifully conventional Catholic. But during the Sixties he got irreligion: the Church had failed on the big social issues of racism and sexism, and he began to think for himself. "Now," he recalls, "my mind was racing." Evidently it raced very fast, for his thoughts are still a blur. He asks, with the triumphant air of Perry Mason trapping the perjured witness, why babies, who don't ask to be born, are stained with original sin; how an all-loving God could allow His Son to die on a cross; whether Martians would need salvation; and other stumpers. Take *that*, Aquinas.

Clearly, a man in his mid-forties who would settle for this facile schoolboy stuff *wants* to settle for it. At about the time his intellect attained its present splendor he was making a lot of money and not getting along with his first wife; but do you think leaving Catholicism was the easy way out for him? Guess again: "I thought … about the void and how much harder it is to rebel than to just 'go along.'" We have his word for it.

Vanity apart — he remains our foremost Philophiliac — his ruling passion is anti-Catholicism. He accuses the Church of being "destructive," of "retarding growth, inhibiting my ability to reach out." (Phil is big on growth, and quotes an assistant's confession that "working with Phil Donahue has been one of the most growthful experiences in my life.") He can hardly go three pages without a sneer at his erstwhile religion.

Now why is this called "leaving the Church"? We don't say a boy has left home if he goes only as far as the front lawn, and there turns around to throw curses at his parents. The point of leaving is to leave something behind, to go elsewhere. Donahue has to keep proving he isn't an altar boy any more, as by televising an abortion.

By way of establishing his moral and intellectual credentials, he attacks racism, sexism, the military-industrial complex, business corruption, and (what guts) Richard Nixon. Every liberal *cliché* comes with the air of an annunciation:

- "We should not use crippled children to sell hamburgers. Ever."
- "Today's mother is caught in the most dramatic shift in mores that has befallen any women in history."
- "In short, Americans don't like the news, and like the angry impatient king, they are beheading the messenger."

He doesn't see that his present vociferations are as tamely conventional within the media as his old formal piety was at Notre Dame. He's still playing it safe: a moral chameleon. And even when confessing his sexist insensitivities he's flaunting his new awareness of them. (All self-censure, said Dr. Johnson, is oblique self-praise: it shows how much you can spare.) But he has the fundamental insensitivity of the egotist: he can talk only about himself, and all the people in his life are mere wraiths to him. No reader of his book could accurately describe any of them.

Meanwhile he continues in his mission of doing for the housewives what my old professor did for us, the brightest generation in history: by example and ridicule, teaching them to subdue their common sense in favor of mass-media liberal proprieties of perception, concern, speech, and behavior. Helping, in his little way, to make God taboo, with heaps of altar-boy earnesty.

# The Sage and Serious Doctrine of Hugh Hefner

*February 1, 1974*

> *Fain would I something to say, yet to what end?*
> *Thou hast nor ear nor soul to apprehend*
> *The sublime notion and high mystery*
> *That must be uttered to unfold the sage*
> *And serious doctrine of virginity.*
> — MILTON

Twenty years ago, *Playboy*'s first issue hit the newsstands. Now a photo review of the Playmates reminds one of the magazine's lean years. Few girls, and fewer pretty ones, were willing to pose nude in those days. The first issue featured Marilyn Monroe in the famous calendar poses of *her* lean years, rights to which, as all the world must know by now, Hugh Hefner had bought for peanuts; and in subsequent issues, the *pretty* Playmates were often called upon to do encores. One, in fact, was Playmate of the Month three times, and also served as the magazine's subscription editor.

Despite the girl-next-door aura that helped make the Playmates famous, many of them, those early days, had a rather self-conscious fallen woman look about them; rather like the girls in other girlie mags, like *Rogue* and *Dude*. You know the pose: breasts thrust forth, tummy sucked in, legs coyly crossed — and the face, oh the face! What it lacked in beauty, it made up in ardor and mascara. Come hither, reader, it said — chin up, mouth open, tongue between bared teeth, eyes half open but gazing right at *you*, mister, and yes it said yes — though she looked like a girl who, off camera, chewed gum and said yeah, that Playmate of yore.

If the Playmates have changed, the captions have changed more. They have always been aloof, but they used to be more humorous. Though Gloria, or whoever, might look ecstatic with desire for the reader, the caption would just ignore that, according her instead something of the detached admiration that is the meed of fine horseflesh — she was described in fancy phrases like "amply endowed," "pulchritudinous,'" "cantilevered,'" and "39-21-35.'" The jocose circumlocution was necessary, for *Playboy*'s specialty is not merely sex but also attitudinizing about sex, putting it in a comforting setting of sophisticated camaraderie.

The difficulty of writing texts for such pictures is greater than one might assume. Try it. What can you say: "The reader will note that Gloria has huge knockers"? No. No! You have to be more elegant than that, or why say anything? And *Playboy* has this compulsion to say *something*. It has, easily, the largest words/knockers ratio in the history of girlie magazines, and that ratio helps account for its success.

*Playboy*, after all, is about success. It's almost a success manual in the guise of a girlie mag. And success means more than prosperity: it means *respectable* prosperity. "What sort of man reads *Playboy*?" the ads run. "A young man on a direct course to success." Young men can look to *Playboy* for all around *savoir faire*: it shows them not only what to wear, but what to say, and (not least, in a society so devoted to verbal one-upmanship) what to sneer at (bluenoses and Nixon are among the safest targets). It's easy to scoff that the Playboy Philosophy wouldn't sell without the nudes; the point is that the nudes wouldn't have sold nearly so well without the philosophy.

That philosophy — consenting adults and so forth — is by now widely accepted as respectable, if not simply axiomatic. What other porno magazine could feature panel discussions on ethics, with photos of the earnest, thoughtful faces of Ivy League theologians? (Not too long ago it would have been thought indecorous for a clergyman to show his face in even such harmless men's magazines as *True* and *Esquire*.) It is fairly common, nowadays, to hear Catholics, even priests, say they don't want to "impose'" their "views" on the rest of society, not even their "views'" on whether a human fetus is a human being. That so many people should think their own deepest convictions are merely "subjective" is a measure of Hugh Hefner's … success.

The philosophy is no longer a regular part of the magazine, but it is briefly reformulated here and there: "Not coercing or injuring others is, we believe, essential to a free society. Beyond that minimum, we view morality as an individual matter, a highly personal belief in what is right or wrong." And it pops up in occasional editorials, like the one that scolded the Supreme Court for its obscenity ruling:

"The obscene is a subjective concept, existing only in the minds of the beholders ..." — the sort of sentence that will at last drive a teacher of freshman composition to leap from a bridge, though it is always uttered triumphantly, with obvious confidence that it cannot be answered. Moreover, the same editorial affirms, "there are ultimately 200,000,000 qualified judges of obscenity in the U.S. and ... each has a right to his opinion," raising the question: what can "qualified" possibly mean? or "obscenity"? or "right"?

The difficulties are plain enough, and I don't mean to belabor them. But *Playboy* is not even consistent. State laws making fornication a crime, for instance, are "a shock to the conscience." An odd way for *Playboy* to put it: *the* conscience? How does *the* conscience differ from all those "personal," "individual," "subjective" consciences? Is there a Higher Law obligating Rhode Island to let its citizens rut at their pleasure?

I'm being silly now, of course, because what is important about such a remark as I have just quoted is not its substance, but the act of making it. Any young man on a direct course to success knows the value of gestures, including the occasional gesture of by-God indignation. *Playboy* knows what to shake a fist at, as well as what to sneer at. There are fashions in morals as in everything else, and the magazine's trend-setting instincts are so good you'd swear that men of the cloth were as eager to pose for it as the girls are.

Still, *Playboy* has to be careful how it gets indignant; it is paradoxically inhibited by its own libertinism. When, in a survey of current porn films, Contributing Editor Bruce Williamson tried to put his foot down, there was nowhere to put it. Straight and even gay films were okay with him, but films of bestiality and sex with children were, he said, "weirdo junk" which "even dedicated swingers" "might" find "hard to stomach." He didn't go so far as to call for police action, or even to speak of a "shock to the conscience" (Williamson is no bluenose). He couldn't: he could only sniff, mustering up the withering contempt of the tastemaker, that kiddie and doggie sex are sort of infra dig, or infra dog, as the case may be. Weirdo junk indeed, frowned on by the right people.

Inhibitions have fettered even the captions of late; so that, ironically, as the pictures have grown more explicit, the captions seem to be trying to change the subject. *Playboy* has been sensitive to the charge that all that "amply endowed" stuff reduced women to sex objects, and accordingly Gloria or whoever is now discussed strictly as a Human Being, and pictures of her ample endowments are accompanied by straight-faced texts about her PhD candidacy, or her aspirations as an actress. A recent issue featured Sacheen Littlefeather, the alleged Apache who refused Brando's Oscar for him; the captions movingly described the formation of her social conscience. It seems she used to be ashamed of her Indian heritage. Then, four years ago ... A remarkable human being, Miss Littlefeather. To speak of her as "cantilevered" would be a shock to the conscience.

The magazine's "native" prose is wearyingly *jejune,* like the captions. The film reviews, for instance, aim at a tone that is both hip and authoritative, trying hard to sound as if they must be taken seriously; the reviewer never fails, even in the one-paragraph review, to glance self-consciously back over the director's *oeuvre,* just so you know he knows there's an *oeuvre* back there — he seems to be writing to gain the approval, or at least to escape the contempt, of better critics, rather than to guide the reader. The overworked adjectives — "provocative," "controversial," "masterful" — bespeak the reviewer's feeling that he must somehow deliver a verdict he doesn't really know how to reach. And this feeling is the natural result of *Playboy*'s doctrine that "value judgments" are "subjective," like sexual preferences. If there are indeed 200,000,000 "qualified" judges of obscenity, nobody is really more qualified than anyone else, and no rational aesthetics is possible. *Playboy's* taste in movies, books, and music, as in women, is bound to be shallow and watery; "respectable."

"My taste in women," says Hefner in an interview in *Playboy's* twentieth anniversary issue, "isn't exactly a personal aberration; it happens to be shared with some 26,000,000 *Playboy* readers." That is the remark of a man waiting in line at the world's biggest gangbang. Tom Wolfe has observed that Hefner is "king of the status dropouts" — he couldn't have, and didn't aspire to, conventional respectability, despite his enormous success, and so he has created his own society, his own world, centered around the Playboy Mansion in Chicago, complete with its own ideology (the Playboy Philosophy). Hefner doesn't even think of himself as a businessman primarily (he says businessmen tend to bore him), but as a cultural force — perhaps it's more accurate to say, a countercultural force. A liberal, but the friend of radicals. He proudly claims friendships with

Martin Luther King, Jesse Jackson, Lenny Bruce, Linda Lovelace; and his name-dropping earns him a sort of respectability-by-association. *Playboy* even carries relatively udderless pictorials of parties at the Mansion, just so you can see that Hefner does enjoy a certain status, that he moves among celebrities — but only celebrities of culture.

Ironically, Hefner is just the sort of mass cult figure who must be disowned by the intelligentsia who aspire to *real* respectability. So *Rolling Stone* has lately put him down, hilariously, and so has Garry Wills, subtly. Though Hefner says *Playboy* is, literally and otherwise, the best magazine in the whole world, Wills, a frequent contributor himself, pooh-poohs such talk and says it's simply the best girlie mag ever, period. Wills is the kind of urbane soothsayer who helps give it what quality it has; his contempt is barometric, and seems not to have gotten him in Dutch with the magazine, which now features him more often, and more prominently, than it did before his backhanded tribute.

Despite his outspoken "Gospel" Catholicism, Wills makes it clear that he thinks *Playboy,* if not meritorious, at least innocuous. "I have nothing against nipples," he says, defining the issue with his usual precision. But he could be worse: he could be Harvey Cox. A few years after his famous attack on *Playboy* (in his book *The Secular City),* Cox underwent the most remarkable conversion since Saul set out for Damascus, and published in its pages a synthesis of Playboy Philosophy and kerygma. Jesus, he announced, "was *not* an ascetic," but a social revolutionary who loathed prudes, was indulgent toward "what some considered to be … adultery," and was, after all, the guy who supplied the "booze" at the Cana wedding. Besides, Cox said suggestively, who knows what he did between the ages of 12 and 30? Needless to say, Cox also charged that the churches have systematically distorted Christ's message — a theme as congenial to *Playboy* (and as gracious to his own co-religionists) as Wills' sneers at Catholic priests as "mass-produced eunuch servants to the church bureaucracy." How sublime to hear these two discourse on the Church's prophetic mission of rebuking a sinful world!

The general banality of *Playboy* reflects the banality of Hefner himself. This is made obvious in the long interview in the anniversary issue, an interview which took six months to compile and edit, and whose fruits include *aperçus* like this: "Open, healthy sexuality requires that we not be ashamed of our own bodies." And this: "I think nationalism is a dangerously outmoded idea, and we ought to start thinking of ourselves as one people living on this little planet together." And furthermore: The Supreme Court's ruling on obscenity was "totalitarian," and liberals who aren't up in arms about it are "being very shortsighted, and they remind me, quite frankly, of the good citizens of Germany who felt it didn't have anything to do with *them* if the Jews had their rights taken away." (Linda Lovelace said the decision reminded her of Hitler, coincidentally.)

*Playboy*'s anonymous editors, however, are well pleased with the interviewer: "He saw all of this complex man's facets and explored, more thoroughly than we dared hope, his thinking." And the interviewer is well pleased with his subject: being in Hefner's presence, he says, is "a forceful, funny, absolutely extraordinary experience. Like his legend [what legend?], Hefner is larger than life, [an] elusive, contradictory, sometimes maddening, sometimes just mad genius," who has "all the facility and polish of an uncommonly shrewd politician," and, but for his "tremendous reserve," "could be a very successful stand-up comic"; moreover, "in many ways, he is an even more remarkable figure than his legend [*what* legend?].... The man is 47, but his energy is staggering ... his powers of concentration are — well — overwhelming.... His mind is so quick, so totally focused ... an incredibly compelling personality..." He despairs of getting the full impact of his experience on paper.

Hefner, for his part, tells us that his salient qualities are "idealism" and "skepticism of bullshit," implanted in him by his parents, and nourished by films like *Mr. Smith Goes to Washington*, films about heroic loners who question the accepted "'truths'"; whence his own sense of mission about challenging "'truths'" like the one that says it's naughty to go around without any clothes on, and his indignation against those good-German liberals who won't march against the gas ovens with him. "In the liberal's history book," Willmoore Kendall has written, "it is always Socrates and the Assembly, always Socrates who is 'right' and the persecuting multitude that is wrong. Always, therefore, Socrates must be *saved*, retrospectively and prospectively, from the Assembly, which *ex hypothesi* brooks no disagreement with its 'truths,' and forever thirsts for the blood of those who presume to disagree with it." To the liberal, ordering society rightly means, finally, insuring that "Socrates can *go on talking*."

Or selling feelthy postcards. Or otherwise participating in that great process of self-subversion that is the Good Society.

But enough of Hefner the thinker. What of Hefner the man? He confides to his 26,000,000 readers that his success has enabled him "to get laid a lot." And yes, "I've been personally involved with a number of our Playmates over the years.... There does seem to be a rather high correlation between our most popular Playmates and those who have been most important to me personally." (So *that's* the legend.) The same issue features pictures of past Playmates, with captions telling you which have been the most popular.

Hefner's own brand of conspicuous consumption appears in the way *Playboy* frequently shows his favorite ... consenting adult ... Barbi Benton. The first time, five years ago (back in the days when Sacheen Littlefeather was still ashamed of her Indian heritage), she was introduced as "Rising Star Barbi Benton," naked. Though she has so far risen only to minor appearances on *Hee Haw,* clad, the magazine continues to display her with a rather pathetic doggedness; somewhat like Orson Welles, as Kane, insisting that his poor bride *shall* be an opera star. The parallel isn't exact; Hefner's devotion seems unlikely to consume Barbi; and of course they aren't married (Barbi calls it a "mutual discovery relationship," or something). Still, the whole Barbi thing, like the interview, shows the extent to which *Playboy* is given to indulging Hefner's private vanities.

Hefner says that *Playboy*'s cultural impact means more to him than all the money he has made — and no doubt he means it. He is proud of the rich variety of contributors he collects; the anniversary issue offers stories and articles by Nabokov, Bellow, Updike, Galbraith, O'Faolain, Wills, and others, boasting: "Never let it be said that *Playboy* does not serve the whole man." And what sort of whole man reads *Playboy?* Again, the ad answers: "A man for whom success is no accident.... And this man's life has many facets. Not surprisingly, he finds all of them reflected in his favorite magazine," his multifarious appetites conveniently ministered to by the juxtaposition of Vladimir Nabokov and Barbi Benton. The sort of man who, before there was *Playboy*, subscribed to both *The Atlantic Monthly* and *Dude*.

The sort of man, at any rate, who likes to think all those things true of himself. My guess is that *Playboy*'s typical reader is like Hefner himself: self-consciously tasteless. He buys it because it gives him not only what he likes, but also — flatteringly — those things he feels he *ought* to like, even if he doesn't. Taste, of course, means more than just liking the Right Things; it means a sense of the fitness of things, that intelligent instinct which, if he had it, would prevent Hefner from publishing, e.g., nude shots of his beloved Barbi (though this may be his idea of gallantry), the fawning of some of his own staff (in the context of which even his modest remarks heighten, rather than diminish, the comedy of self-congratulation), and a "philosophy" which tears sexuality out of the social order (thereby reducing it to sterile rutting), and which denies, in its inability to distinguish between the erotic and the aesthetic, the very possibility of taste (thereby reducing art and literature to the status of trivial and extraneous adornments of life, rather than creative and ordering activities). "If a bull could speak," says Dr. Johnson, "he might as well exclaim, 'Here I am with this cow and this grass; what being can enjoy better felicity?'" Hefner is an oddly deferential bull in the china shop of culture; a bull, indeed, who collects china. And whatever a Nabokov may be in himself, to a Hefner, and to the sort of man who reads *Playboy*, he can be no more than a fancy piece of bric-à-brac — like a plaster of paris Rodin, sitting off there in the corner, imparting an incongruous hint of class to the gaudy mansion of the most pretentious meatpacker in all Chicago.

# Gone With the Whip

*March 4, 1977*

Of the printed reactions to ABC's *Roots,* the most interesting is that of Roger Wilkins. Mr. Wilkins, now an editorial writer for the *New York Times,* is perhaps best described as a former Negro who suffers from the delusion that he is still a Negro, and that every thought he thinks is accordingly a genuine black thought. The truth is that he is really a white liberal, with all the parochialism and even ethnocentrism of the breed.

The three episodes of *Roots* that I saw were uneven but irresistible. How fitting that its ratings should rival those of *Gone with the Wind,* whose romanticization of the old South it complements by romanticizing slavery. The slaveowners are shown as uniformly cruel and stupid, but that is less implausible than the ennoblement of the slaves by their captivity. The trouble with systematic oppression is that it does debase so terribly, making its victims (except for the saints) mean and cowardly. Yet the blacks of *Roots* keep their dignity intact, leading a psychic double life, Tomming it for Massa, but, among themselves, secretly and indomitably proud. It has been charged that *Roots* played on white guilt, but I doubt it: how could one feel that these valiant sons of Africa had been essentially and permanently harmed? Their shuffling is all an act, their hearts remain pristinely leonine.

We are nowadays instructed to despise "stereotypes," but organized minorities demand that they be publicly depicted in "positive images." Wilkins acknowledges that *Roots* "has been criticized for some historical inaccuracies" — presumably of mere detail — but he contends that "they are as nothing compared with" the myths it displaces: *Roots* is "substantially closer to historical *and psychological* truth" than those old myths (my emphasis). This is quite unbelievable. The most remarkable thing about Alex Haley's family is that it managed to preserve its genealogy all the way back to Gambia; I know of no other black family that has done so. The sheer social indignity attached to being black has surely done more harm to Negroes than any merely material injury inflicted on them. This, I think, is the "psychological truth" of our racial history: that whole generations were made to grovel, with lasting consequences for their descendants. The value of *Roots* is that it imaginatively provides American blacks with a legitimizing lineage, a therapeutic myth and beneficent stereotype acceptable to both races, fostering black self-assurance while actually minimizing white guilt. The cruelties of whites in *Roots* are so monstrous that not even Lieutenant Calley could feel organically related to them. Those evils are 'way "back there," so egregious and discrete from routine racial snobberies as to let us all off the hook.

Though he admits it is unfair to blame today's whites for slavery, Wilkins presses his point: "The white vision of humanity has been so pervasive that it did indeed warp black people's perceptions of themselves." Spoken like a true son of the West, and particularly like a *Times* moralist. This remark identifies "white" with "vulgar white racist." Like most liberals, Wilkins assumes that Western universalism is universally shared. What, one wonders, is the Mandinka word for "humanity"? Or "equality"? Or, for that matter, "racism"? Perhaps the best way to suggest the "white vision of humanity" — the one that has prevailed — is to recall that the sentence "all men are created equal" was written, and urged upon the world (the white world) as a truth that ought to govern political arrangements, by a white man. A white slaveowner.

The very terms in which Wilkins lectures us are "white." So is *Roots*. It was produced by white executives who bet eight nights of prime television time that other whites would watch a serial that, superficially, portrayed their race unflatteringly. If we are, as the Garry Willses charge, "a racist society" (headed for "the second civil war"), the capitalists haven't heard about it.

On the contrary, we are a liberal society. The very concept of "racism" depends on a "vision of humanity" peculiar, as far as I know, to the civilization we have inherited — and preserved. Most people in this world are narrow and tribal, fearful of aliens, thinking of their own races as specially favored, chosen, destined to rule others. We Westerners may be proud of, and grateful for, the patrimony that teaches us to regard all men as endowed with rights. To be sure, all men want freedom — at least for themselves. But not all men want freedom for all men. To suggest that white men are unique in their residue of tribalism is to get everything backward. We are really distinguished by the extent to which we cherish the human capacity for transcendence. For all his excesses, even a Garry Wills is a credit to his race. Ditto Tom Wicker, and Roger Wilkins. They are only a little parochial in thinking that all men would turn out like us, if only we left them alone. But liberals are made, not born: tolerance is not genetic, but environmental.

White Americans, notes Mr. Wilkins, "were once capable of treating gross cruelty as the natural order of things." In this indignation there is a deep complacency. There is so very much gross cruelty in the world that only recently has it occurred to people to try to abolish it: to institutionalize kindness, so to speak. A noble aspiration, yes — but to presume that it is feasible to do so, let alone "the natural order of things," is naïve. People who flee slavery and tyranny are usually grateful to get away with their own hides. Abolitionism is as a rule beyond the scope of their imaginations.

Perhaps the best way to bring the point home to a liberal of Mr. Wilkins' stripe is to point to refugees from the Soviet bloc. How many of them think in terms of doing away with Communism? Are they encouraged by the likes of Mr. Wilkins and his colleagues at the *Times* to think of the Soviet regime as something other than the natural order of things? Most people know that evil is here to stay, and that they can do little more about it than to weed their own gardens. It is hard enough to secure a small area of peace and order.

Margaret Mead, that queen mother of liberalism, has observed that "under the manifest fear of miscegenation lies the knowledge that all forms of cultural behavior can be lost, that they are dearly purchased and dearly kept." And it was Edmund Burke who told us that we can ascend to universal charity only from a base of loyalty to the "little platoons" of our origins. The value of *Roots* is not that it has much diminished ordinary human narrowness and irrationality — which Mr. Wilkins seems to suppose are monstrous aberrations (he is *such* a liberal) — but that it has established a desirable social fiction, one apt to encourage a concrete historical bond of affection of white for black Americans.

# Mass on the Mall

*November 23, 1979*

I took my two older children — Kent, 13, and Vanessa, 12 — to Washington for the October 7 Mass on the Mall, but the only good look at the Pope we got came the day before. We arrived on Saturday afternoon and joined the crowd on Pennsylvania Avenue waiting to see him come away from the White House. We easily found a place on the curb — the crowd was that thin. But I let Vanessa sit on my shoulders to make her even more visible than her bumblebee-striped shirt already made her.

He came within thirty feet of us, looking craggier than in his pictures but just as genial. Vanessa insisted later that he had cupped his hand as he waved our way in response to her cupping *her* hand, individualizing his greeting in a split second.

He passed quickly, cruising among the temples of modern bureaucracy. The crowd dissolved. Some feminist protestors began dismantling a stand they had erected to protest the sin (mortal or venial?) of sexism. A swarthy foreign priest, with black tangled beard, was wearing a button that said, "Start ordaining women — or stop baptizing them." One woman handed me a flier and said kindly, "This explains what we're trying to do." Another woman gave me another flier. She had a strange combination of garments on and I took her for some sort of nun, but she turned out to be a Seventh Day Adventist warning against a collusion between John Paul II and Edward Kennedy. The idea was to turn the country Catholic, the most enlightened program yet associated with the name of Kennedy.

Two newlywed friends of mine put us up for the night, and we had beer and pizza and salad and homemade ice cream, and argued gloriously together against enemies who, luckily for them, weren't there. And so to bed.

We were up before dawn and at the Mall by nine. Thousands of people had arrived before us (some had camped there overnight) and occupied hundreds of feet of space between ourselves and the huge altar. We staked out our own territory and settled down in a bright sun with a slight chill. The sun left; the chill stayed. By noon it looked like rain.

The crowd, where we were, was subdued. The whole number was only about a third of the 600,000 predicted. It was hard to tell who was Catholic and who was just curious.

Myself, I'm an on-again, off-again Catholic. Lately I have been on again. This Pope is part of the reason. His constancy in a life of sacrifice and peril both shames and inspires one who has wavered between God and fun. Now he has emerged from the trials of Poland to tell Catholics in the West that their sacrifices matter. The faithful here — scorned and ignored by the cultural interpreters who dominate public opinion — feel recalled to life. And there must be many like me, to whom the word "faithful" hardly applies, who are moved to rejoin them. It is as if the Church and some of her marginal members have come out of retirement together.

At three o'clock the waiting became a countdown. A priest stepped to the microphone at the altar to lead the saying of the rosary. The crowd stood as if unanimously Catholic and chanted rumbling responses. One felt a sudden sense of imminence.

When John Paul II arrived there were no hysterics, not even much excitement, just a massive intentness. Mass began swiftly. It seemed less a meeting than a reunion.

The sermon came over the loudspeakers in solemn Slavic cadences that made me think of *Ivan the Terrible*. It was strange to hear those sounds in Washington, headquarters of the New Class that reshapes American life during the week and spends Sundays in the suburbs. Here was a different class of people, profaning earth consecrated (so Madalyn O'Hair insists) to undefiled secularity.

All week long John Paul's speeches had been getting nearer and nearer the heart of Catholic doctrine. Now, in his final address, he was saying the things even most of the faithful shrink from saying openly, even when they believe them in their heart of hearts.

"And so, we will stand up every time that human life is threatened."

"When the sacredness of life before birth is attacked, we will stand up and proclaim that no one ever has the authority to destroy unborn life."

Every *r* was an obstacle; every *i* prolonged, so that words like Christ and life seemed to have two syllables — a felicitous emphasis.

"When the child is described as a burden or is looked upon only as a means to satisfy an emotional need, we will stand up and insist that every child is a unique and unrepeatable *gift of God*" — his voice rising with plangent conviction.

This was the part of the sermon liberal voices would take as the "hard stuff," dogmatic Catholicism at its worst. And clearly John Paul had not crossed the ocean to recant on behalf of his Church. But I was glad Kent and Vanessa were hearing it, hoping they would understand what he was saying about them, about the children they will have: that children must never be subordinated or sacrificed to lesser goods.

Hedonism has its own prudery, ashamed not of vice but of virtue. I have never understood why people are so resistant to conceding anything to the Church's position on birth control: in my unbelieving days it was one of the things that made sense to me, since it was not involved with supernatural allegations. One reason there are so many teenage pregnancies is that young people sense, whatever their elders say, that the act of love, even when illicit, is somehow corrupted by selfish calculation. Margaret Sanger has become a secular saint, but in her day she aroused nearly universal indignation, offending a sense of fitness few will now admit they possess. Why are the *liberals* so inflexible on contraception?

John Paul was speaking the very nearly unspeakable, defying worldly authorities as truly as he ever did in Poland. These were words that were worth crossing an ocean to utter. No doubt they came as a rebuke even to many of the faithful, and I was gladder than I had a right to be at hearing them. But even those Catholics who disobey the Church aren't necessarily defying her. Most of them know they are part of the world too, and they need, even in their weakness, to know they can turn to someone who stands apart from that world, speaking to it rather than with it. I felt less that he was infallible than that he was right. Even if I were still an atheist I would have felt it awesome there, in the capital of enlightened wheeling and dealing, to hear the voice of an ancient order in which things do not, finally, submit to manipulation.

# That *Commonweal* Girl

review of
***Catholics and American Politics***
(Harvard, 262 pp.) by Mary T. Hanna

*February 22, 1980*

This book costs 15 bucks. I say this by way of admonition, not self-pity: I got it for free. But then I had to read it, and you don't.

Boredom is hard to quintify — I mean to type "quantify," but I must have been thinking of quintiles or something, since this is one of those books that back up their assertions with charts and tables and dauntingly bedecimaled percentages. Anyway, boredom is hard to *quantify*, so I can't express my reaction to this book in the categories preferred by the political scientist, Mary T. Hanna, who wrote it. She goes in for Agree and Disagree — things like that. Nothing in there about Snore.

*Catholics and American Politics*: good title, necessary topic. I just read *Commentary*'s symposium "Liberalism and the Jews," and while I can't say I had the time of my life, it is at least true that the respondents were invited to think, and some of them did so. But Professor Hanna elicits stock answers in her interviews and *insists* on stock answers in her polls. For instance, Table 4.14 poses the question, Do you "support civil liberties for" atheists and Communists? White Catholic college graduates who attend church less than monthly: Agree 96.6 per cent for atheists, 93.1 per cent for Commies. No figures are given on how many of the respondents, or for that matter how many of the editors of Harvard University Press, replied, Just what on earth is *that* supposed to mean?

This is less a book than a symptom. Its real aim (the author doesn't evidently possess the focus of consciousness that would justify accusing her of concealing it) is to show that Catholics are Making It. That is to say, Becoming Liberal. To Become Liberal you don't have to ask distracting questions like what "support civil liberties for" implies. You just have to say *Yes*, or better yet, *Yes!* though of course Table 4.14 can't record exclamation points.

Now as a matter of fact I don't know how anyone could say *No* to the question as phrased. Some of my best friends are atheists, and I certainly want them to have "civil liberties" as I understand them (though how Professor Hanna understands them is anyone's guess). Beyond that, I feel that no Communist should be strung up without a fair trial. Does that qualify me as a supporter of "civil liberties" (in the Hanna sense) for Communists? Or do I have to believe that they also have a right to equal employment opportunity in the FBI and CIA?

Then there is the little matter — if it's not extraneous to raise the subject with respect to an assistant professor of political science at the State University of New York, Binghamton campus — of Professor Hanna's prose. I can't give you the quintiles, but here is a typical sentence: "However, the areas of agreement seem wider than those of disagreement." Here is an even more typical sentence: "Both Church and congressional leaders stressed continuing Catholic support for economic liberalism and, indeed, survey analysis showed Catholics to be consistently supportive of governmental problem-solving efforts in education, health, the environment, big cities, and so on." And so on. Hell, have a couple more: "White Catholics also demonstrate a dramatic rise in their levels of support for civil liberties guarantees. Thus, they bear out Church and congressional claims of a greater Catholic openness and tolerance toward others, with all the implications that development of such attitudes have [*sic*, I guess] for political participation and its modes." Also, Professor Hanna is fond of beginning sentences with also, comma.

If you read between the lines — which in this case sure beats reading the lines — you quickly see, as I was saying, that the point of the book is to congratulate "educated" Catholics on their achievement of Correct Attitudes. Would you believe it, they come out better — i.e., more liberal — than Protestants at the corresponding levels of education? Why, I'll lay odds that mentally retarded Catholics come out better than their mentally retarded Protestant counterparts. Again, I don't have the quintiles to prove it. Also, I have a hunch that if you screen out the Baptists, the Catholics will fall behind again. (Or from another point of view, come out ahead again.)

Which is a way of saying the less "educated" people are, the more likely they are to retain a measure of common sense, since they are more immune to the social pressure of "educated" opinion. State education has boomed since World War II, especially at the college level, and with it the power of liberal orthodoxy. In the old days a Catholic was likely to go to a school where he learned the substance of his faith and how to defend it; he was inoculated against at least the obvious secular fads. More recently the Catholic schools have withered, and many Catholics have rushed eagerly out of their ghettos to assimilate, even if it has meant forgetting how to think. Writers like Professor Hanna and Andrew Greeley labor to prove that Catholics now a) retain distinctive Catholic values, and yet b) are more like other people than other people are.

Meanwhile, others — Baptists, for example — have carefully kept their distance from the public mainstream. And in their way, they have preserved habits of disciplined thought that the assimilated have traded for respectability. Professor Hanna betrays a paradisal innocence of the possible implications of "government problem-solving efforts." But I recently happened to hear a fundamentalist radio preacher give an extraordinarily incisive analysis of the real meaning of the current campaign for "children's rights." Nobody can presume to say which will more likely enter the kingdom of heaven, but that preacher was certainly fitter than Professor Hanna to converse with James Burnham.

The *Playboy* ads used to ask, "What kind of man reads *Playboy*?" The answer, of course, was an enviable man — young, educated, motivated, sophisticated, and all that. As part of its style package *Playboy* offered political uplift: it taught Correct Attitudes toward issues of the day, which attitudes were always quick-frozen bits of liberal dogma. You didn't have to do any thinking; you simply put the relevant attitude on like a hat, and presto! you were fashionable.

That is how opinion is now communicated through the media, and in its dreary way Professor Hanna's book belongs, albeit unwittingly, to the whole system of opinion marketing. Its title is the best thing about it, but a better title might be *What Kind of Person Reads Commonweal?*

# Memoirs of an Unsung Hero

review of
***Memoirs of a Dissident Publisher***
(Harcourt Brace, 260 pp.) by Henry Regnery

*August 3, 1979*

This book acquired a terribly ironic epilogue after it was printed. Having given his life to losing causes, Henry Regnery confesses toward the end of *Memoirs of a Dissident Publisher* that he has always lacked the tragic sense of life: "Life has probably treated me too well for me to develop a philosophy of my own…. That our Maker feels kindly toward us, his creatures, the music of Bach and Mozart would be for me sufficient evidence, if there were not much more."

Then, in Chicago's disastrous DC-10 crash, he lost two key men in his little firm. One of them was his son Henry.

Young Henry did his father proud, and spoke proudly of him. Whether or not he lived to see this book in print, he surely knew its contents. They are ennobling. Henry Regnery Sr. is one of the unsung heroes of the conservative movement, playing a thankless, inglorious, financially precarious role in seeing to it that some of the seminal books of conservative thought got into print at all.

In publishing as in few other lines of endeavor, virtue is pretty much its own reward. Regnery's father cautioned him, "If you ever begin to make any money in that business you are going into, you can be pretty sure that you are publishing the wrong kind of books." After studying engineering at MIT and economics at Harvard, Regnery, an ardent young New Dealer, spent a disillusioning summer in Washington working in the Resettlement Administration. He also spent two years in Germany, absorbing its culture, when Hitler's new regime was still background noise. In the Forties, after a brief stint in his father's textile business, he got into publishing by something like accident.

He met Frank Hanighen, who, with Felix Morley, was about to launch the newsletter (as it originally was) *Human Events*. In association with them he arranged to publish pamphlets from his

Chicago home. But they couldn't maintain actual editorial control over such a distance, and his operation became independent. After the war he put out a few books critical of the Allies' occupation policies in Germany, which weren't a large improvement on American policy toward Japanese-Americans in California. For a time he tried to claim nonprofit status for his company, but the IRS nixed that — without instructing him, however, in the ways of making profits. In order to appease market forces on IRS terms, he was forced to supplement books defending the market with occasional offerings like *The White Sox Year Book*.

For the rest, it was an adventure. He introduced writers like Russell Kirk and William Buckley; imported for the first time Max Picard, Raymond Aron, and Romano Guardini; published unfashionable books by Charles Beard, Victor Gollanez, Wyndham Lewis, and Ezra Pound when other publishers were afraid to touch them; brought out surefire non-best-sellers like a three-volume edition of Thomas Aquinas' all-but-unavailable masterpiece *On Truth*. His other authors included Morley, James Burnham, Willmoore Kendall, James Jackson Kilpatrick, Frank Meyer, and John Dos Passos.

The book abounds in anecdotes of these men and the circumstances of their publication. Lest their books be forgotten, Regnery gives concise summaries of them, full of memorable short passages. The Regnery name became a red flag to liberal reviewers, who could be counted on to snub or abuse with fair regularity any book bearing it. He quotes many of these reviews, so damaging to both his firm and the causes he served, and thereby achieves, at least, dramatic historical vindication: his authors maintained a remarkable level of prescience about everything from Soviet behavior to the future of Social Security.

Even his successes had perverse consequences. *God and Man at Yale* created a national sensation, but it moved the Great Books Foundation to break its contract with Regnery, wiping out profits from the book and a sustaining backlist of classics in the process. A book of photographs of Palestinian refugees resulted in an FBI "investigation."

Regnery devotes a whole chapter to Russell Kirk and *The Conservative Mind* — a book that has undeservedly gone out of fashion even among conservatives, but is clearly close to its publisher's heart. The most colorful chapters deal with other conservatives, notably

Kendall, and with four great men of letters: Campbell, Lewis, Eliot, and Pound, who remarked to him: "One must find a way to admit one's mistakes without throwing away the glimmering of truth one has managed to acquire in making them." Such moments, and there are many of them, make Regnery's autobiography a valuable document on the life of the conservative mind.

# Those Who Can't

review of
***Capitalism: Sources of Hostility***
(Epoch Books/Arlington House, 206 pp.) edited by Ernest van den Haag

*April 4, 1980*

Ernest van den Haag knows when argument is futile. In this he differs from most arguers of comparable brilliance (and he will forgive me for talking as if there were any). He once debated Ramsey Clark on the death penalty and performed an invaluable act of locating and spearing the ideological impulse: after Clark had gone on about how capital punishment doesn't deter crime and therefore doesn't save lives, van den Haag put it to him simply: What if it did? Would you then support it? Answer: Negative. Even so, the lesson was lost on its intended beneficiary: the patient proved incurable. Clark still lurches from forum to forum opposing the death penalty. If he can't be deterred (though has anyone really tried?), he certainly can't be rehabilitated either. He is a walking self-refutation.

In *Capitalism: Sources of Hostility*, van den Haag confronts the mystery of why the most vital economic principle is so widely and bitterly hated, denied even the empirical credit it deserves. He and his fellow contributors to this little volume offer a range of answers, most of which may be summed up in one word: envy.

It isn't easy to say where moral passion (or moral confusion) leaves off and envy begins. Obviously some people deserve to succeed. Just as obviously success tells us little about desert. The market doesn't satisfy the deepest moral yearnings but it does chafe envy. Van den Haag writes wittily and trenchantly on this theme, particularly as it has to do with intellectuals — who tend to want to remake the market on an economic model, *à la* Harvard, where promotion matches desert and envy is a stranger.

Envy is now widely confused with covetousness. But to covet another's good is to want to possess it yourself; to envy it is to seek the darker satisfaction of destroying his happiness in it. Iago is the envious man, and recent criticism has found him an enigma because it has tried to understand him in Benthamite terms.

The generations who lived before the Enlightenment had no trouble understanding or recognizing envy. It was one of the seven deadly sins, and old authors like Plutarch and Shakespeare write easily of it as a basic human motive. (In Plutarch, Brutus kills Caesar out of envy; in Shakespeare, he is the only conspirator *not* driven by envy. Shakespeare's alteration simply points up his shared sense of the vice's distinctness.)

Capitalism excites envy because it makes people responsible for their own economic fate — less at the mercy of chance, bad weather, and the like. In principle, modern enlightened people should like this, because it rescues us from subjection to fate. But in fact it doesn't happen that way. For many people the naked responsibility is unbearable, and they hate those who do better than themselves. Several of the contributors to this volume — van den Haag, Roger Starr, Lewis Feuer — suggest that intellectuals tend to be men who have chosen intellectual pursuits partially out of fear of economic competition. The collectivist and communitarian ideologies they embrace are often rationalizations of personal insecurities. To paraphrase Shaw: Those who can, produce; those who can't, call for the socialization of the means of production. (Not much of an epigram, but I'd memorize it if I were you.)

This seems to me to explain a lot about the temper of, say, many of the folk who write for *The New York Review of Books*. It goes without saying that capitalism is dehumanizing; all discourse is organized around that taboo. Accept that, and you can ignore the bloody-fanged malice and the egoism, raw or feline, of all those types who screech about Community and the Humane Society. (Let's give her her due: Ayn Rand had their number long ago.)

Several contributors point to the strange rebellion of so many children of capitalism. It's an old paradox by now: the more pampered, the more self-pityingly rebellious. Van den Haag reminds us that children used to be "investment goods." One reason for having kids was so that they could help with the family farm or trade. Today children are more like — get this — "pets." They are a luxury; and this is not an altogether happy status for one's moral and mental health. Craving moral assurance, they like the kind of moral authority a socialist system pretends to give, telling them they earn what they get. The impersonality of market rewards, however great, cannot mother them this way.

And why does the Third World, which ostensibly craves basic development, hate capitalism so? Peter Bauer thinks it's because of a peculiar warp in the whole system of communications between the West and the rest. Rulers of "emerging" nations like planning, of course, because it helps consolidate their power. But even beyond that, according to Bauer, *only* the advocates of collectivism have managed to get through to the Third World — in most of which a free economy is hardly thought of as conceivable, let alone moral or practicable.

"What the Third World learns from the West, or about it or about present and past economic relations between the West and Third World countries, comes from or is filtered through opponents of the market. They dominate international reporting, the wire services, documentary films, and entertainment." Bauer recalls lecturing widely in India around 1970, and finding that his rather orthodox economics were hardly intelligible to his university audiences, to whom it was self-evident that central planning was best, the sole question being whether the Soviet or the Chinese model was more appropriate. They took for granted not only that planning was necessary for development, but also the idea that socialist policies "promote or even imply social and economic equality." Most startlingly, perhaps, Bauer notes that although British colonialism was rather lax throughout most of its history, in its last years it imposed increasingly socialist structures on its colonies. "As a result, the ready-made framework of a *dirigiste* or even totalitarian state was handed by the British to the incompetent independent governments."

I've meant to convey that these are stimulating essays. Also worthwhile are those of the other contributors: Nathan Glazer, Dale Vree, and Stanley Rothman. Not so good is the binding, which split in the copy I was reading, though I understand other copies have held up well.

# Up to Liberalism

review of
***Confessions of a Conservative***
(Doubleday, 1979, 231 pp.) by Garry Wills

*May 25, 1979*

America's gifts to literature include a special kind of autobiography: the memoir of cultural assimilation. Since the days of Edward Bok a newer kind of "Americanization" — from subculture to mainstream — has been the theme of books like Mary McCarthy's *Memories of a Catholic Girlhood,* Norman Podhoretz' *Making It,* Claude Brown's *Manchild in the Promised Land,* Larry L. King's *Confessions of a White Racist.* In each, an author of acquired urbanity looks back at his provincial origins, recalling the struggle of transcendence, the pain of forging a new self. Nostalgic or derisive, he looks back with detachment, since such a book is itself a way of validating the new self by exchanging the "we" of kinship for the "they" of citizenship. The genre addresses itself to the society he has "made it" in rather than the one he has left behind. The common pitfall is a failure to maintain enough detachment toward one's own success, a temptation to mistake conformity to a new society for the achievement of autonomy.

Garry Wills has had more than one past to transcend. *In Bare Ruined Choirs,* where the memoir was oblique, the "ghetto" was Catholicism, the old faith of beads, prayers, miracles — an irrecoverable home of an old self of naïve faith. The new, urbanized self found fulfillment in an "underground" Church of "doubt," where unseemly supernaturalism was replaced by ecumenical social protest. Scorning both frumpish traditionalism and crude trendiness, muting doctrinal particularity, Wills appeared to be saying that the "underground" Church had somehow been the "real" Church all along. Nevertheless, I read that book with an uneasy sense that he had made enormous and needless concessions to the cultural pressures he nervously disparaged. The price of his loyalty to Catholicism, as he defined it, was apparent in a remark of Phil Berrigan's about the Church, quoted by Wills with tacit approval: "She's a whore, but she's our mother." The stance was a curious *defensive* trendiness, too eagerly incorporating the attacks of Catholicism's "cultural despisers."

In *Confessions of a Conservative* the ghetto is, disconcertingly, *National Review.* Wills began writing for *NR* in 1957, when he was 23, and the first quarter of this book recalls his decade as a regular contributor. Though this phase of his career is embarrassing to him, he writes about it with love and candor; his portraits of Bill Buckley, Willmoore Kendall and Frank Meyer bring them right into the room.

Subsequent fallings-out seem only to deepen the affection of these chapters, and the remarkable thing is the way Wills preserves the sheer romance of his first dizzying day with "the world's greatest blarneyer," who whizzed him around town and country and capped it all with a compliment that seemed outrageous at the time: "What a day for *National Review* when it gets both Whittaker Chambers and Garry Wills." If that kind of treatment doesn't sweep a Midwestern lad off his feet, nothing will. But Wills' warmest memories are of Meyer, "the world's most gregarious eremite," and his wife, Elsie. Wills and Meyer shouted away many long nights at Woodstock, reading Shakespeare and arguing politics with an intensity that made Elsie intervene. She needn't have worried: the friendship survived Frank's principles and Garry's heresies, and these pages are a beautiful votive candle to it.

It was through Meyer for the most part that Wills dealt with *NR* and the Right in those days, and his overgeneralizations about conservatives today — rigid individualism, racial anxieties — are probably extrapolations from the Woodstock shouting-matches. Like Meyer, Wills actually had little part in the magazine's internal life. Hence two of its three main presences, Jim Burnham and Priscilla Buckley, are oddly wraithlike in his account, while Bill Rusher, publisher since 1957, isn't mentioned at all. Sometimes he is just wrong, as when he offers as plain fact his rash guess that Bill Buckley's connection with *NR* is by now merely nominal. Since Wills hasn't been in these parts for a decade, one would think he might, as a journalist, have inquired.

This makes for intellectual gaps too. It is strange that Wills fails to notice features of Jim Burnham's thought that he ought to find quite congenial: "elitism," anti-utopianism, a conservatism of loyalty and givenness, what might be called strategic resignation. To speak of the Right's "messianic anti-Communism" without a nod to Burnham's style of thought (he wasn't messianic even in his Trotskyist days, much to Trotsky's dismay) is to engage in caricature.

Wills rightly stresses the influence of Albert Jay Nock on the original *NR* crew, many of whom came over from *The Freeman* (in its postwar incarnation). But he presents Nock only as the effete poseur, which is right but not relevant. Nock the man wasn't around. Nock the thinker deserves a little better. He predicted gloomily that World War II, however it came out, would principally mean the advance of totalitarianism (a word Wills avoids — significantly, I think). And it is worth noting that for Nock the opposite of "state power" wasn't (as for Meyer) individual rights, but "social power." Conservatism's rhetorical emphasis on individualism is not so antisocial as Will believes. It is also strange that he brushes by John Chamberlain and Henry Hazlitt, only to repeat a canard no reader of theirs should be guilty of: that market theory is fallacious because we've never had a free market.

Stranger yet is his talk of right-wing "theocracy." It is hard to know what he means. He even dismisses Eric Voegelin as theocratic — the opposite of the truth, as he should have known from the phrase "the immanentization of the eschaton" which was so often cited, and played on, in *NR* during the years Wills wrote for it. Had he read Voegelin carefully, he would have known that his own Augustinian notions of the limits of politics were no novelty to conservatives. He might also have realized that those notions don't necessarily lead one to the position he has reached. Instead he tends to assume that his differences with others are largely due to his having read things they haven't.

In fact, as he draws away from selected friends and speaks of the Right as a whole, Wills increasingly abridges and cartoons its positions. The reason is not any evident malice or inherent obtuseness, but the needs of dramaturgy. He is writing about himself, and he recalls the Right, here, as a misty mise-en-scene, the Way We Were, consisting (like the ancient faith of *Bare Ruined Choirs*) of Things It Is No Longer Possible To Believe. This is a contemporary tale of the Self's Progress, and *NR*-style conservatism serves as a backdrop for that self's Growing Doubts. Its credenda are not to be refuted, but outgrown; he is not speaking to the old tribe, but about it, to an audience with none of the tribal commitments he "confesses" having shared, and who won't mind inaccuracies about those commitments.

But he is "confessing" in another sense too. Though he has left our parochial parish, he has not left the church itself: he is still, he insists, a true conservative, in a deeper and broader sense than those he has left behind. The rest of the book dramatizes his emergence, and concludes with a personal credo of great eloquence. But one step at a time.

The memoir fades out early, as Wills recalls leaving the *NR* fold something of an "ideologue" (though Meyer cannily sniffed heretical tendencies from the start) to become a genuine political journalist with *Esquire*. He quickly excelled as a reporter and caught (and was caught by) the fever of the mid-Sixties riots and demonstrations. It was then, he says, that he actually began to see how America really works: the main result of observing the 1968 campaign was disillusionment with the electoral process. But he was already too wise to be soured by the reality; instead he decided we needed a theory to do justice to the system's real (as against its alleged) virtues.

Our elections, he says, don't really affect things all that much; a candidate must have appeal so broad as to blunt any meaningful principle. How, then, are we governed? By mutually controlling elites — businessmen, bureaucrats, even prophets — who are reconciled by another elite, the politicians. Nor does he disapprove. He thinks the whole contraption works well enough to be worth putting up with, serving competing values tolerably and for the most part humanely. He defends it (wants to "conserve" it) against the streamlining efforts of ideologues who yearn for the total ascendancy of any one elite, of any obsessive principle.

There is some purposeful debunkery in this: Wills wants to snuff out self-righteousness about the American Way, lest we fall into messianism. In fact he stresses structural resemblances between the American and Soviet systems. Both, despite official professions, are forms of "state capitalism." Ours is far better, though both are guilty of historical brutalities. Here he lapses into asymmetries in quest of symmetry. He mentions our victims (blacks, Indians, etc.) and doesn't specify theirs; he equates our "critics of the Gilded Age" (Mark Twain et al.) with their "dissidents"; we "seized lands" whereas they "absorbed adjacent territories." He admits but minimizes differences between Soviet and American elections: "Ours are better managed, not to say stage-managed. There is less restraint on political initiative in America." He doesn't bother mentioning the *forms* of restraint; they are subsumed under grandiosely abstract concessions: "Admittedly, there were [*sic*] injustices in Russia and China, massive and terrible." But we too, in the name of anti-Communism, began taking on Communism's features — "secret police," and all that.

A bit facile, this, since our secret police never ambushed individuals, let alone millions, with instant death or terminal sentences to slave-labor. As he says, "elections reflect an ethos rather than create it"; but he ought to consider the way a system can, in turn, distort the ethos — especially when the system itself wipes out huge strata of the population. Wills still thinks in categories like national character and historical guilt, apparently failing to understand that totalitarian rule is essentially discontinuous, a largely technological kind of mass-control that can annihilate vital traditions. He sees the Soviet system as a kind of variant of old Russian "authoritarianism." No doubt it derives from old Adam too, but that is only a partial (and not a specific) explanation. There is a curious sense in which he seems impelled to assert that all regimes are somehow representative of their nations, as if peoples were naturally led, as by an invisible hand, to the rulers they deserved.

The source of this error is not itself an error, but a sound insight: what he calls "the family as the basis and model for society." The last section of the book restates his theory of "the convenient state," appealing to St. Augustine, his intellectual hero. Augustine held that it is not justice but earthier affections by which men are united in society. Only God knows what each man justly deserves, and this will be revealed to us at the end of time, not before; meanwhile the citizens of the two final cities — of God and of the earth — must live together indistinguishably in the "peace of Babylon." The state performs a less than eschatological function; it must not presume to do God's job of separating good men from bad.

True. But Wills is surprisingly vague about the pertinence of all this to his own position in American politics. The best he can do is suggest that our "crusading anti-Communism" (his gift for fresh phrase deserts him here) caused us to try to "administer final justice around the world," as in Vietnam. But if we were so fanatically anti-Communist, why, during that war, were our leaders courting improved relations and "détente" with the Soviets and, later, China? Why were they so eager to negotiate an end to the war?

The fact is that we aimed not to destroy but to "contain" Communism — a policy that was formed in the years when, the Soviets having absorbed adjacent territories (and others adjacent to the adjacent ones), we perceived that we were as Indians to their Manifest Destiny. A misconceived strategy, perhaps; but still a strategy, and not a demonology. Wills forgets his own cogent objections (in *Nixon Agonistes*) to fighting a war for the procedural goal of free elections in which the very enemy we were fighting might win: such a goal, absurd as it is, was at the opposite pole from "final justice."

I think there are two basic confusions in his theory. One is a failure to distinguish between state and society. The other is a failure to distinguish among kinds of justice, so that he is forced to shuttle terminologically between (mere) "justice" and "final" (or "ultimate" or "perfect") justice. In one sense, a limited state (an Augustinian legacy, by the way) can promise "to establish justice," meaning not final rewards but simply just civic relations.

These confusions cause Wills to see all states as organic and more or less familial extensions of their subjects, and also allow him to blink the specific evil of totalitarian regimes. As James Hitchcock puts it, the persecution of Christianity by Communism — official denunciations, exclusion from jobs and schools, removal of children from believing parents, imprisonment and forced labor, torture, murder — is the "dirty little secret" of liberal Christians, a subject unworthy of mention in the urbane society to which books like *Confessions of a Conservative* are addressed. Wills makes light of formalities like elections as criteria of a regime's virtue, but he never raises the first question Augustine would ask; never reflects on the consuming nature of a state that resents the worship of God as an affront to its own claims; never regards such a state in the light of Augustine's insistence that no peace is possible between the citizens of the City of God and the persecutors of Christianity.

This omission seems to me to trivialize his invocation of the saint, making it merely a fancy warrant for a modish anti-anti-Communism. Not that *The City of God* supplies us with a foreign policy. But whatever our practical policy toward anti-Christian regimes, surely we must *talk* about them, even — especially — in company where it makes us squirm to do so. That is a very light burden to bear, considering the daily ordeals of our less privileged fellow Christians. Yet Wills treats any such concern, when he thinks of it at all, as kid stuff: "I had grown up a Catholic cold warrior, praying after Mass every day for the conversion of Russia, rallying to anti-Communism around that cold-war icon, the statue of 'Our Lady of Fatima'" — as if wishing Christ on Russians were something akin to bombing them back to the Stone Age.

The book's very last chapter is a subtle, apolitical meditation on the self. Again drawing on Augustine, Wills develops the theme that "one is never more oneself than in the extension of the self." Even repentance implies self-love, in that we love "the recoverable self of possibility," we move forward through the love of "a yet unknown self," progressively discovered by knowing and transcending past selves. Though drawing on religious imagery of creation, its subject is man's "creativity," capacity for "growth," and "endless possibilities." As a comment on the relation between continuity and renewal, it is most impressive (so is a passage on *The Odyssey* that precedes it). Coming at this point in *Confessions,* it also invites us to admire the "performing self" that has acted out its own possibilities in this literary pilgrimage from one conversatism to another.

The performance of that new-renewed self is always stylish and often brilliant. But there is something too pat and self-congratulatory in the pilgrim's progress from an unfashionable conservatism he refuses to call conservatism to a fashionable liberalism he refuses to call liberalism. The appeal to Augustine is a weak basis for a convenient solidarity with what is assumed to be Enlightened Public Opinion. It is the achievement of that solidarity, an achievement portrayed as a self's lonely voyage, that is the real subject of this book. Ironically, Wills seems not to see that he has written the kind of story he has so often mocked: the success story of a self-made man.

# Martyr-In-Chief

*February 20, 1981*

I happened to be watching TV at 3:30 A.M. on Jimmy Carter's final day in office — eternal vigilance and a touch of insomnia being vital to the TV critic's calling. At that hour a bulletin informed us that the President was still up too, waiting for the last hostage hitch to be straightened out.

Even my hard heart softened a bit to learn that Carter hadn't been allowed one last night's sleep in the White House. Those Iranians really are a bit much. Of course Carter did everything possible to bring his woes on himself, but — "use every man after his desert, and who shall scape whipping?" (Khomeini's avatars may have taken those words in the wrong sense.)

Carter wanted desperately to clean this mess up before leaving office, a mess that epitomized his Presidency. I felt I knew him too well even before our Embassy was taken. But since then, we have been saturated with the most intense TV coverage of both him and the "hostage crisis." The two were made for each other.

What more fitting preoccupation could Carter have than this agony of his own making? And we watched him all the way through it, right up to the end. He used the media more than any President ever had, used them to break down barriers of formality between his office and his people: the fireside chat in the cardigan, the radio phone-in, the frequent press conferences, the town meeting.

He kept a pollster by his side too, thinking that was the way to maintain contact. While lusting for popularity, he nonetheless complained that he wasn't appreciated when he made unpopular decisions.

He always seemed to want cameras present. He wanted intimacy with 226 million people at once. He wanted them to behold his virtue. He said he'd never lie to us — and on the night of the election, when he conceded, he reminded us that he had said that, obviously believing he had kept that pledge. And maybe he had.

He liked us to see his suffering, too. He wanted us to know how personally he took the travails of our hostages. Their well-being became his top priority, never mind the well-being of all the potential hostages exposed to danger by the very stress he put on personal safety.

That distorted perspective threw an ironic light on his farewell address, when he complained of single-issue and special-interest groups. Having no philosophy of his own, he had no grounds for resisting immediate pressures from any quarter. As James Fallows observed, Carter had an opinion on everything, but no sense of how to integrate his views. He remained oddly undefined: he had conscience without character, scruples without principles. The special-interest group that finally brought him down was in Teheran.

In the long run Carter proved a very trying TV *object*: his slumping, rubbery looks, his feeble, off-key voice, his total lack of charm, magnetism, and eloquence now make his defeat look retrospectively like an aesthetic inevitability.

In Carter all the lofty prescriptions of liberalism found a dismal embodiment. Don't use force, don't antagonize anyone, renounce our past and our allies. TV showed us these propositions incarnate in one little man who struggled to outgrow a Georgia background that should have been his strength: he was trying to move up to liberalism just as the rest of the country was trying to cast it off. Didn't he ever notice that he had won the Presidency by looking fairly conservative?

It got wearisome, too, hearing him repent of other people's sins: racism, Vietnam, Watergate, and general lying. He would lead us out of the distorting fear of Communism that had involved us in so many unsavory alliances. He would embody national repentance in dealing with Panama, Zimbabwe, and Iran itself. Groveling was even in our interest: it was a form of plea-bargaining with the future, that stern socialist future in which Third World nations, coming into their own and realizing their "legitimate aspirations," would sit in judgment over us.

Having worn out his welcome in our living rooms, Carter had the misfortune to run against the greatest TV politician yet. No doubt he and his advisors felt, reasonably enough, that he had to debate Reagan; and he may have even outpointed him on the so-called "issues."

But it's clear by now that the debate sealed Reagan's victory. With one superb stroke — "There you go again" — Reagan dramatized, made real and visible, what the country was sensing: Jimmy Carter was small.

I can think of five splendidly theatrical moments in the campaign, and they all belonged to Reagan. The other four were the microphone grab in New Hampshire, the gentle, funny putdown of priggish John Anderson in Illinois, and Reagan's last two half-hour broadcasts. The one on election eve brought tears to my eyes. But the previous one, on the economy, was a masterpiece of what liberals call the "simplistic"; that is, it was concrete, incisive, and irrefutable.

Intellectuals, who live by playing up their intelligence, don't understand Reagan. He lives by playing his down. He may be despised for being an actor, but he has a genius for empathy: he can reach people, putting his thoughts in their language for them. To call him simplistic is simply simplistic.

# Mindsets

*December 24, 1982*

As I watched CBS's half-hour special on the death of Brezhnev, I felt that for once I was getting close to the heart of American liberalism. The program wasn't "pro-Soviet"; it made no attempt to glamorize the Soviet Union or even to portray Andropov as a closet liberal. Dan Rather was evidently trying hard to tell it straight, and Bill Moyers was nowhere to be seen.

One clip showed Ronald Reagan at his first presidential press conference, saying that there was bound to be friction between the two superpowers as long as the Soviets reserved to themselves the right to lie and cheat. Then there was another clip of Reagan at his recent press conference discussing Soviet efforts to infiltrate the nuclear-freeze movement. A CBS correspondent remarked that this showed Reagan still had the same "mindset." Hasn't changed a bit.

The condescension of it! Reagan takes Lenin at his word: the Communist isn't bound by "bourgeois morality." And putting Leninist doctrine together with Leninist behavior, he concludes that certain difficulties are posed thereby for those who seek peace; whereupon the shapely blonde journalist notes with mild alarm the peculiar Reagan "mindset."

Even the shots of Brezhnev's funeral were reminders that the Soviet Union is on a war footing. Martial music, goose-stepping soldiers, Andropov's inaugural bluster: but all this can be dismissed as mere "rhetoric," never mind whether it squares with Soviet actions.

With my friend Tom Bethell, I have taken to referring to the world socialist community, including American liberals, as "the Hive," the metaphor implying that there is unity in all the diversity, even as there is unity among all the spontaneously differing bees in a bee-hive. Some people have thought we are suggesting that liberals are crypto-Communists. Not at all. On the contrary, we are suggesting that they are best understood as what might be called *para-socialists.*

That is, they never criticize socialism in principle. It is less a matter of idealizing socialism (whatever that would mean by now) than of failing to appreciate our own institutions or to see an incompatibility between those institutions and the superstate. The garden-variety liberal in fact tends to blame conflict on those who *think* there is conflict, as Reagan does; he tends to see our institutions as defective and dispensable, rather than good and worth defending. For this reason we never hear it suggested that the Soviet abolition of private property is downright evil; ditto the Soviet subjugation of the family and persecution of religion.

Instead there are bland references to "our differences," along with hints that these are not really so great. We have leaders, they have leaders; we have nuclear weapons, they have nuclear weapons; we have an economy, they have an economy. The two superpowers are fundamentally analogous. Even Afghanistan is their Vietnam. Same thing.

The Dan Rathers can and do freely criticize the Soviet Union, but at a preposterously superficial level. The Soviets are guilty of "human-rights violations" against a few dissidents; their economy is crippled by "rigid central planning"; but, well, that's about it. Even these, on the evening news, don't seem much different from our own prosecution of Dr. Spock and the flounderings of Reaganomics — with the additional distinction that however clumsily the Soviet economy is managed, nobody will be heard accusing Yuri Andropov of making "war on the poor."

Dan Rather lamely tied up the Brezhnev obituary with one of those where-do-we-go-from-here questions: Can Andropov balance the demands of "the Soviet military" against those of "the Soviet consumer"? That remains to be seen. Good night.

Well, I have seen the Soviet consumer. He stands in long lines in the cold waiting to spend a bit of his meagerness on a chunk of discolored meat or a small roll of toilet paper. The Soviet consumer is no match for the Soviet general. And sporadic food riots don't add up to a Ralph Nader movement; if a Muscovite throws a rock at the police, he isn't going to be *Pravda*'s new media pet.

Yes, there is a mindset problem, but it isn't Reagan's. It's the mindset of those who drone on about "our differences" without the slightest grasp of our real differences. Dan Rather would probably locate the distinction between the two superpowers somewhere in the neighborhood of the First Amendment. Our press is free; theirs is "censored." Leaving aside the triviality of a free press compared with the enormity of unfree religions, "censored" puts *Pravda* in the wrong category. It is not as if the Kremlin stifles the journalistic energies of *Pravda*: the Kremlin *supplies Pravda*'s energy. The Soviet press is an organ of tyranny, not a victim of it.

The greatest irony of all is that we have a President who understands the differences, while his media critics simply don't. They try; they try to be even-handed, to avoid bias and jingoism and gullibility; but they're out of it. They have eyes, but they see not; they lack the imagination to see fully the things they gaze on. They are too uncritical to be good critics; and too unappreciative. If they don't know what the Soviet Union is, it's because they don't know what the West is.

The most lamentable failure of critical imagination is to call Brezhnev a failure or to say the Soviet system doesn't "work." That system does what it's supposed to do. Brezhnev did pretty much what he set out to do. And one thing he set out to do was to create the kind of confusion that is the mark of American public opinion, as represented by Dan Rather.

# James Burnham, 1905-1987: Editor, Thinker, Colleague

*September 11, 1987*

Jim Burnham was so refined and restrained that I nearly fainted the first (of two) times I ever heard him use a vulgar word.

A State Department official had just announced, with moral pomp, that the U.S. was withdrawing recognition of Rhodesia. I found Jim alone in his office on a quiet midsummer day. He commented: "Sometimes in this world you have to throw your friends to the wolves. But you don't have to talk a lot of shit about democracy while you do it."

That impressed me, because Jim was rarely one to vent indignation. Just the opposite. The other editors might be assembled like Agamemnon's council, shouting and banging their spears on the big conference table; Jim would sit, quiet and still, listening calmly as the furies spent themselves. Finally Bill Buckley would turn to him: "What do you think, Jim?" And we bangers and shouters would hush to hear the gentle rasping voice restore pertinence.

Jim appeared undistracted almost to the point of indifference. He smiled and laughed, but he was never one of the boys. His expression was typically concentrated and quizzical. To a reader his mind might seem cold, though his personal manner was always considerate.

I couldn't figure him out. It would have embarrassed both of us if he'd realized how intently I was studying him. I read and reread his books; they puzzled me too, though *Suicide of the West* had changed my way of seeing the world. His thought had a simplicity achieved by shedding the irrelevancies that obsessed others, including conservatives.

Burnham was interested in the logic of power. His method was to look at everything in the world from the angle of its power-value. This made the moralist in me squirm, especially since he regarded even morality under the same aspect. At times, with a few mild critical questions, Jim could make me feel like a sentimental, attitudinizing liberal.

So I was fascinated by his own rare shows of anger: they disclosed a deep sense of honor, otherwise hidden like shame. George Orwell missed this (a natural enough mistake) when he accused Burnham of worshipping power. Jim didn't worship it; he did unsentimentally respect it, and he came to terms with it in his own way, without compromising his honor. Later, Orwell more perceptively saluted Jim's vision and courage, and made the geopolitics of Jim's early books the premise of *1984*.

*The Machiavellians* is the key to Burnham's thought. It sets forth his analytical principles so plainly — almost brutally — that it takes a stern mental effort to adjust to them; in order to grasp them you have to resist the normal temptation to import all the "values" he has eliminated. I took years getting the hang of this.

Jim did like to shock. *The Machiavellians* belongs to the same period as "Lenin's Heir," a piece he wrote for *Partisan Review* to "*épater les Trotskyistes*," as he told me once, smiling. He épatered them, all right. He called the holy martyr Trotsky a "Platonic Communist" and said that Stalin, not Trotsky, was Lenin's true successor. Far from "betraying the Revolution," Stalin had fulfilled it in its real essence: power.

Burnham made a cardinal distinction between those who know what they are doing and those who don't. "The difference between Henry Wallace and Gromyko," he remarked in 1948, "is that Gromyko knows what he's doing." For him that was the basic difference between any liberal and any Communist.

Liberalism and Communism, he saw, work toward the same *telos,* and though their notional goal is a fantasy, together they form an order in the realm of power. This could and did happen without liberals' fully realizing it; Burnham tried to deprive them of what he felt was their culpable innocence. Their relation to Communism fascinated him like a spiders' mating dance. You couldn't apprehend the Communist phenomenon without understanding its liberal paramour, the submissive partner offering herself in sweet surrender. To the liberal, this was the world well lost; to Burnham, it was the suicide of the West. His sovereign eye seized the pattern of the twentieth century and made it shockingly obvious. Even now the world keeps enacting Burnham's thesis, as falling apples vindicate Newton.

He never burned to make converts. His titles were apocalyptic — The *Struggle for the World, The Coming Defeat of Communism* — but his prose was more analytical than oratorical. You could accept it or reject it. He knew how he'd had to earn his own vision, how much it depended on his own experience, readiness, personality, and luck. He was too fatalistic — too Marxian, maybe — to think that mere brilliance could infuse it into other men. If your way of seeing things happened to overlap with his, he might reach you, and that was about all he hoped for. He expected to be largely ignored by a preoccupied world.

He had been prominent enough in his day, until he unforgivably offended the respectable Left — not the sort of thing a power-worshipper would have done — by refusing to indignate against Joe McCarthy. Then he was ostracized. I never heard him express the slightest bitterness about this; he'd known what he was dealing with — History, on a certain scale — and I don't think he took it personally.

He seemed quite content with his perch at *National Review*, from which he could speak with all the freedom he wanted to those who had ears to hear. He wasn't a lapel-grabber, after all. Life's options were always more or less narrow, and the art of living was to exploit the givens. "If there's no alternative," he would say, "there's no problem." Don't curse fate; just look for the available pressure points. He exercised his own kind of power, the leverage of words cunningly chosen and timed. But some of those words survive their contexts with inexhaustible implications.

# Censorship, Stereotypes, and Other Fine Things

*July 21, 1978*

Art in our day has acquired a special charisma, and many consider censorship a sacrilege against its dignity. I think I love and respect the arts as much as the next man, and I have always thought myself a native of this country, a rather typical native. Yet when I hear the tones and accents of veneration with which many of my countrymen speak of Art, and the unqualified and unexplicated contempt with which they refer to Censorship, I feel like a foreigner, an uninitiated tourist, who has failed to grasp the inner meaning of terms whose obvious senses cannot account for the values and emotions attached to them.

Television, for instance, is getting racier, which leads many to say it is getting freer. The fare of *Three's Company* and Johnny Carson's monologues is the sort of thing that used to get movies C (Condemned) ratings from the Legion of Decency. Such private ratings belong to an ill-understood realm between pure libertarianism and state suppression: the realm of social inhibition, etiquette, things that Just Aren't Done.

The great majority of inhibitions are implicit, almost unconscious, and it is even a sign of their precariousness when they have to be stated. A few years ago it would have been unthinkable — never mind illegal — for a girl to walk down the street with her breasts visible: as it were the moral equivalent of flashing. It was not that young women had to be reminded, or had to decide, to dress decently every morning. Nor would any American except an anthropologist have thought to mention covering the female bosom as one of our customs. It was just second nature, one taken-for-granted aspect of a larger system of decorum, based on deep-rooted notions of what human nature is, with derivative habits of propriety that were assumed by millions who had never had them spelled out. Now law, armed with force, is necessary, but in general it is really the backstop of custom; when it has to be too widely enforced it isn't much good. Most people break some laws, but still it is true that most people don't even think of breaking most laws. An effective censorship has to have the support of consensus in morals and manners.

But, as I say, censorship is a thing of bad repute among us. Taboos are taboo: our very selection of the non-Western word sprinkles the vinegar of irony on any open attempt to control expression. Yet there is obviously a good case for controlling it, as long as we admit that people's sensibilities matter. The idea that there should be no taboos or censorship is part of liberal ideology and rhetoric; the reason being that the forces of liberalism arose in opposition to traditions that had long been defended by censorship and other sanctions. Hence the liberal tradition has always associated itself with free expression *à outrance.*

But this principle is unrealistic, and its universalism is perforce specious. Ideals, to be established, have to be supported by more than mere arguments, more even than habit. They require sanctions, including, in one form or another, censorship. Now that liberalism is in many quarters the established faith, it employs these sanctions too. But since it disguises from itself its recourse to controls it affects to scorn, it thinks "thought control" is what the Right does to the Left. When the Left (defined for present purposes as anything liberals regard as a progressive force) does it to the Right, it is something else. Conservatives have a rich literature, and a richer gossip, of tales of liberal discrimination against votaries of other points of view — in academia, the press, the media, and private society.

When I taught English composition in a Midwestern university, for instance, I was once accosted by an older professor with whom I had never discussed politics: he snapped that he understood I was a follower of William Buckley and the John Birch Society ("You left out H.L. Hunt," I replied), and what the hell did I think I was doing in a "liberal university"? That was my only unpleasant experience in a wonderfully good-natured English department, and it hardly qualifies me for martyrdom; but the sense of proprietorship with which he spoke is eloquent as to the real and perceived pecking order of ideas. (So, in a way, was the gentler kidding I often got.) Obviously a great many things go into academic hiring. Let's just say that for a prospective teacher liberalism doesn't hurt, and conservatism doesn't help, even when these things are not decisive, or even inquired about. Academicians are seldom inquisitors. Still, they tend to see liberalism as the common sense of the educated, and almost as an aspect of civilized behavior. When conservatism isn't loathed it is usually somewhat on the defensive, and the conservative has to prove himself not to be a fascist, in somewhat the way, in certain right-wing strongholds, a liberal has to prove he has no sympathy with Communism. In that respect liberalism is an orthodoxy.

Up to a point people have a right to their prejudices — which is to say that they may, and should, see to it that their convictions get appropriately institutionalized. Liberals do this, naturally, as much as the rest of us, only better; better because they are under the necessity of deceiving not only their enemies, but themselves. And the most interesting (because most fundamental) part of what we call liberal "bias" is not what they do to us, but what they do to their own.

The Educational Testing Service, just outside Princeton (and not connected with the University), employs a black whose principal task is to bowdlerize its test questions of any material offensive to blacks. I am sure that it has never occurred to ETS officials to call this person a "censor." Rationally, of course, the term fits. But historically, "censorship" has been associated with the suppression of "progressive" ideas and modes of expression. So, for accidental and arbitrary reasons, this office has a different title.

Now ETS — like many such organizations — is not dedicated to promulgating liberalism. It merely pays it an incidental (though sincere) deference. Conservatives must learn to distinguish between the militant liberal — the priesthood — and the larger body of acquiescent liberals — the laity — who have absorbed the creed osmotically, with respect but without any strong desire to propagate it. Liberalism is in a way the "faith of their fathers," and it takes them a specially conscious (often painful) effort of adjustment not to accept it, but to cast it off.

In the arts — really a subdivision of communications — acquiescent liberalism knows it is safer, socially and commercially, to stay on the good side of liberal criticism than to cross it. That is why television, dutifully conventional and dedicated to ratings, feels free to show people as shallow, libidinous creatures, but steers clear of religion (except, as with *All in the Family,* to make "daring" attacks on religious bigotry). Religion is still a real and vital part of American life, but it is amazingly "underrepresented" (to use the liberal term) in mass communications. This is not a matter of conspiracy or even conscious avoidance, but of unconscious habit, much like modes of dress: religion simply isn't in the intellectual wardrobe of media people. Whatever their private beliefs, they know that reference to religious faith would be, if not inflammatory, at least a distracting departure from the customs of the electronic "community." In the Fifties religion-in-general was still a Good Thing. Now it is a darker matter, too problematic to be a natural part of the scene, too jarring to be assumed in the background.

The habits of liberalism create other problems when natives of the liberal culture confront revered parts of the larger Western tradition. Scholars know how anachronistically moderns tend to read old texts; I can hardly bear to see Shakespeare produced, not (I hope) because I am a pedant or a purist, but simply because theater people — liberals all — have no initial sense of the gap between 1600 and 1978; I bridle not only because they misunderstand the plays, but because they seldom suspect that the plays carry insistent meanings that refuse easy contemporary adaptation.

A modern-dress production may be as wildly foreign to Shakespeare as a modern-language production would be. But worst of all is a modern-ideas production. Rather than refuse to perform the uncongenial play, the children of liberalism turn it into something it is not. Julius Caesar becomes Mussolini; *King Lear,* absurdist despair; *The Tempest,* an allegory of colonialism. The director seems to approach the play with the maxim: If its heart offend thee, pluck it out. Don't censor; just "interpret." Filled with the spirit, the performer expresses himself, and his age. He is free. He doesn't stop to think that by ceasing to be the play's humble servitor he impinges on the freedom of the playwright. He becomes the reckless executor of another's will.

This whole style amounts to a claim of irresponsibility for the artist. One of the sonnets complains of "art made tongue-tied by authority"; now we find authority made tongue-tied by art. Joseph Papp is liberated not only from state control, but even from any duty to Shakespeare, who is virtually suppressed by simple ignorance of what he was. The artist becomes the flamen of self-expression and pure contemporaneity, beholden to no older community of art. Of course I refer to the dramatic arts particularly; no orchestra is dedicated to the proposition that its musicians may disregard the score. But of course no man becomes a classical clarinet player if he finds

Vivaldi and Haydn uncongenial. The dramatic arts, however, deal with words, and the words of the past can be thornily alien to the present. Rather than attack them frontally, modern production has defanged them with a strategy of reverent misprision. In this way the theater censors its own.

A few years ago ABC gave us the British National Theatre's production of *The Merchant of Venice,* with Milord Olivier as Shylock. This became the occasion for John O'Connor, the *New York Times'* shrewd TV critic, to ask whether the play should even be presented. You have to understand that O'Connor was not raising an idle or academic question: in liberal, permissive New York, where you can buy *Screw* and its sister publications at most sidewalk newsstands, you won't find *The Merchant of Venice* on the stage, though Shakespeare is bustlingly popular off Broadway. This is, by the way, an object lesson in New York liberalism: things inherently offensive are allowed, but things that offend only a particular bloc are taboo. This is certainly at odds with the professions of liberalism, but yet there is reason in it: the whole can absorb insult better than the parts. Nobody regards the misanthrope as *his* enemy.

After wrestling with the issues for a few columns, O'Connor came down for *Merchant* and against censorship. Two sacred cows had locked horns, and he had awarded Art a split decision. It was really a foregone conclusion. The soul-searching about Shakespeare's putative antisemitism was a necessary ritual, no more. But it was in the tradition of generations of apology for the "barbarism" of our Bard, whose plays so often seem to glorify atavisms like war, patriotism, and revenge, with a silly delight in smutty puns and estranged twins, to boot. Shakespeare's abundance includes plenty to violate the decorum of every age.

And whose fault is that? Shylock *is* offensive. He is meant to be; after all, he is a villain, a man of murderous spite. And the poet links his villainy to his Judaism, setting Jewish legalism against Christian mercy. I don't sneer at those who take offense, but I do smile at an age that can boycott him and still suppose itself all-tolerant — more tolerant, that is, than anyone ought to be. And surely Shakespeare's jaw would drop at the idea that *Merchant* should be performed for an audience of Jews. Only our reverence for Art prevents us from seeing, and saying plainly, that a great work of art can be socially and morally faulty.

How to balance the claims of the aesthetic and the ethical? Always a hard question. But surely we err to hold a simple prejudice in favor of either; and we have no right to demand that conventional morality curtsey to art in every instance. I love *Huckleberry Finn* too, but I can't platitudinize away all those allegedly overwrought Negro groups that object to its portraits of "niggers," and don't want it in the public schools. Of course, Jim is at bottom a noble character, but at a more earthy and immediate level he is a butt. Both Shakespeare and Mark Twain have the gift to turn the stereotype inside out, revealing our unsuspected human affinities with the figures we had come prepared to mock or curse. Perhaps the proper response is for us to see Jim or even Shylock in a new light, though I distrust as sentimental the attempt to redeem Shakespeare for liberalism by making Shylock and Caliban victims. That does not mean we can dismiss the anxieties of people who have reason for concern about the undiscerning part of the audience, any more than the warmest admirer of Orson Welles should disregard or laugh off the panic caused by *War of the Worlds.*

More to the point, the creators of Shylock and Jim, for all their subtlety in portraiture, presuppose the legitimacy of stereotype. They accept, that is, the general perspective of the Elizabethan Christian and the post-bellum white man; and though they enrich it, they don't despise it. We do them wrong to make them crypto-liberals. We also wrong Jews and Negroes to expect them to blithely adopt the perspectives of their contemners.

A stereotype is a conveniently simple image, a recognizable outline. In the dramatic arts it is a character who doesn't have to be explained or elaborately introduced to the audience. The dumb blonde, the wise doctor, the irascible cop: these allow a story to get moving, with a minimum of exposition. Their individuality is of no interest or relevance. They quickly establish audience expectations, a simple function that unique and arresting characters would impede. They serve as background for the real interest of the plot.

In drama as in life, stereotype has to do with prejudice. It represents a preliminary and incomplete, but still valid and necessary, stage in the order of cognition, an early level of abstraction. Since our knowledge is always incomplete and in the process of formation, and our attention is always limited, the fringes of our awareness — the background of our direct attention — must always consist largely of simple and indistinct notions. Johnny and Susie and Billy are unique and precious to their parents, but as they play along the street a man driving by will see them only as an undistinguished group of "kids." He wouldn't doubt that each child has his own traits; but for him "kids" is simply the relevant level of abstraction. The stereotype suffices for this purpose. It allows him to place them instantly in the functional cosmos of the moment.

Of course a stereotype may err, but so may a refined theory. And the economy of awareness and attention demands that we rely on a general sense of shape when we lack time for details. Since we need rules of thumb, it is confusion to talk as if prejudice and stereotype were simply wrong. They are essential to the mind's operation. There is a perspective from which Orientals "all look alike" to Occidentals. This need not be taken to mean that they are all identical, but rather, that to the remote outsider the similarities are more evident than the distinctions. The outsider slips into arrogance only if he assumes that his viewpoint is definitive and all-inclusive, that there is nothing more there than he can see. Prejudice may be reasonable, even when wrong, as long as it knows itself to be tentative; when it refuses any revision, rejects progress toward a shaded exactness, it becomes bigotry.

The stereotype is not merely a matter of individual perception. It also represents social convention: an "established" perception. In a sense, nouns are stereotypes, fixed approximations of varied things. Common nouns, that is. The demand that stereotypes be abolished is a demand that all nouns be proper nouns. A stock character on stage or screen is one whom every member of the audience recognizes at once — and just as important, whom each member is conscious of as equally familiar to every *other* member. The spectator does not say, "I know this character." He says, *"We* know this character."

The commonest reference of stereotype is to races and other minorities and quasi-minorities. As is (alas!) too often the case, our liberal friends have sown confusion in this area. They talk as if their objection to stereotypes were epistemological: as if a generalized perception of a race or sex were inherently unjust to each member thereof. But this is fallacious. From a certain remove, it is virtually tautological to say that a group is characterized by certain traits that distinguish it from other groups. Such traits may be faults or virtues; more to the point, many of them are simply cultural habits which, from the perspectives of other groups, may be variously evaluated. Is group X "loud" or "spontaneous"? "stingy" or "thrifty"? "elegant" or "effete"? "lazy" or "easy-going"?

And naturally our choice of adjectives reflects our own traits. We are as much entitled to our traits as they to theirs. Though it is best to be able to see how any social habit may be either good or bad, it is saner to laugh than to sustain a desiccated objectivity — always provided one admits the right of others to laugh back at us. We laugh at individuals; we also laugh at groups. We may even laugh at ourselves. Nor is it always clear, when we make sport of a type, whether we are laughing at "him," "them," or "us."

Both high and popular art are fashioned from social perceptions. Stereotypes, like platitudes and axioms, are the *topoi* or starting-points from which artists make mere entertainments; but they are also the major premises from which they advance to novel insights, just as philosophers lead us from areas of consensus to deeper, more controversial formulations of truth. All communication involves rhetoric of some kind, and, as Aristotle tells us, rhetoric is based on enthymeme. Persuasion, logical or aesthetic, is not a matter of *fiat* or *ipse dixit*, but of showing us what is latent in what we already know. Where there is no foundation of shared certainty, there can be no further conclusion. Even our prejudices can't be improved on unless they can be shown to be incompatible with other, prior prejudices.

The confused attack on stereotypes has a core of truth: until the Sixties, the Negro was a background figure in American consciousness. This, more than aggressive racism, was the essence of our racial problem, and the major advance in our race relations was our corporate decision that the Negro should no longer be an "invisible man." He came to the foreground, and moved up on what philosopher Joseph Tussman calls "the agenda of attention." But to abolish stereotypes entirely would mean putting everything in the foreground: a mental landscape consisting only of particulars, with no generality. This makes no sense — especially since questions of race involve a level of abstraction between the individual and the universal. Even to speak of "the Negro" is to acknowledge that blacks do indeed "look alike" in various ways.

When liberals ask us to set aside our stereotypes, however, they are usually pleading for idealized stereotypes — "positive images" — rather than for more refined perceptions. The phrase half admits that there are collective traits after all, though it also represents the liberals' failure to look at the concrete features of the very problem they seek to address. And their benign stereotypes fail to persuade us, because the common stereotype has at least a cultural and empirical basis, while the new one they would replace it with is fashioned from sheer hypothesis and hope: it represents the black, woman, etc., they would like to see, not one we can readily recognize and empathize with.

Oddly enough, the older stereotypes are often accepted by their putative victims. Reruns of *Amos 'n' Andy* remained enormously popular among Negroes long after liberal pressure had run the show off prime time. *All in the Family* created a safe stereotype — safe from liberal indignation — of the white bigot, but Archie Bunker belongs to the universe of Kingfish Stevens, farcically unequal to the world's obviousness: except that what is posited as obvious in his world is the truth of liberal ideology, Archie's manifold bigotry being the sole obstacle to social harmony.

But like Vice in the old morality plays, Archie is a more engaging character than the spokespersons for Virtue that surround him. He is at least *real*, and we like him as we laugh at him, though of course we understand that he is perpetually doomed to comeuppance by the decorum of public morality. We like him all the better, in spite of his faults, for lacking the civics-class polish of his children.

After a decade of "positive images," Redd Foxx touched a similar nerve in viewers by being, in *Sanford and Son,* shamelessly, indecorously "colored," shiftless, irascible, with a redeeming Falstaffian resourcefulness, substituting Ripple for sack. He too was deplored by the professional deplorers, who perhaps were only doing their duty; but he garnered a huge and affectionate audience. Affection, as C.S. Lewis reminds us, is the love of things for being merely familiar, like the family; it is an accidental kind of love, treasuring others just for the way they happen to be, not for the way we would wish them; it wants them to stay as they are, enjoys the repetitiveness of their quirks. Dickens is to affection what Dante is to a loftier love, and television is a rather good medium for affection, since it has both incentive and opportunity to give us characters we can like in this way. In that healthy and homely sense, television is conservative.

But it is subject to liberal pressure in many ways. Last year the U.S. Civil Rights Commission denounced TV stereotypes: Edith dutifully fetching Archie his beer, Mary Tyler Moore timidly calling Lou Grant "Mr. Grant," a surplus of black criminals on *Hawaii Five-O*. Liberal editorialists found the Commission's call for federal censorship a bit much, but the jawboning may have had its effect. I suspect, too, that liberals would be more hospitable to censorship if people in the arts, the academy, and the media weren't themselves mostly liberals. Conservatives know from experience how liberal tolerance has meant, in practice, a special hospitality to the Left. Systematic exclusion of the Right from many parts of Academia has made open suppression needless. Most liberals, however, really are tolerant, and in the last few years they have made conscientious efforts, rather against the grain of their preferences, to accommodate conservative opinion — a kind of affirmative action for the Right. Many historical injustices have been corrected, as they say, but the system as a whole naturally continues to favor liberalism.

Why not, really? It is not as if liberalism didn't have deep roots in our culture. The liberal habit of mind comes to us from the Anglo-American tradition of dissenting Protestantism. The most effective way to fight it is not to refute its tenets (that has been done over and over again), but to keep pointing out that it is merely one among many systems of ideas, one to which educated Americans are culturally predisposed in ways that cause them to misread and distort reality. Liberalism, in short, is a prejudice; sometimes a form of bigotry. It has its own stereotypes, from the noble savage to the criminal who is really a victim of social injustice, together with a long line of proto-liberal martyrs of dissent — beginning, anachronistically, with Socrates, who was more like Solzhenitsyn than like Oliver Wendell Holmes.

The mention of anachronism brings me back to Shylock. As Olivier played him, he was a mildly cranky Victorian gentleman, who, after making his final defeated exit, let out an offstage howl of anguish. We no longer have Cibbers and Tates and Garricks rewriting Shakespeare in a frank attempt to reconcile him with contemporary taste. We keep the text — part of it, anyway — and supplement it with stage business that bears no relation to it. Olivier, chief of sinners, has made Hamlet a Freudian study and Coriolanus (dangling by his feet) a fascist. Jan Kott, picking out lines of nihilism, patches together "Shakespeare, our contemporary" — an existentialist, you see. Existentialism is now a bit *passé*, come to think of it, so *that* Shakespeare is no longer quite *our* contemporary.

But then he never was. The honest "improvers" at least had the sense and candor to admit this. Better to see him as a barbarian, sharing (as he did) the prejudices of his time, than to distort him through the prejudices of ours. It is obtuse and arrogant to assume that every great artist of the past must have been an embryo of — ahem — us. That artist, ahead of his time, suffering through misunderstanding, pining for his unborn "contemporaries," is himself a stereotype — flattering to us, no doubt, but blurring lineaments we ought to be able to see clearly. Let Shakespeare have his own stereotypes, and let us look to ours. It may only be our peculiar kind of ethnocentrism — the liberal kind — that causes us to warp *The Merchant of Venice,* when it might make more sense to ban it from the stage.

# Heirs of Elvis

*October 14, 1977*

By the time he died, Elvis Presley seemed terribly old-fashioned by comparison with the current rock scene. How did it get from Elvis to Elton, let alone to sophisticated musicians like Carly Simon and Maria Muldaur, who don't depend on shrieking fans for their sustenance? How is it that rock has remained rock, while offering adult satisfactions never adumbrated in "Hound Dog" or "A Big Hunk o' Love"? Of course he started it, though he can't be credited with all the later refinements.

It is commonplace to say that he came along about the same time Marlon Brando and James Dean became big film stars, that he himself became the focal point of a rebel teenage culture that was, circa 1956, looking for someplace to happen. Commonplace, but true, and relevant.

The striking thing about that rebellion was its rejection of urbanity. Brando might be described as the opposite of John Gielgud. Olivier, with his fire and earth, might have seemed opposite at one time to the ethereal and tremulous elegance Gielgud personified, but the two were really complementary, and could alternate, for instance, as Romeo and Mercutio. Another figure who regarded conventional polish as suspect (or "phony"), J.D. Salinger's Holden Caulfield, complained that Olivier played Hamlet "too much like a goddam general or something." Brando couldn't even have been a private. He was an aesthetic anarch whose advent marked the end of the pear-shaped tone; it would have been incongruous for him to appear on the same stage with Gielgud, though they once appeared in a film of *Julius Caesar* together. They were opposite not as complements, but as incompatibles.

Elvis was the opposite of — well, let's see. Vaughn Monroe, say. His co-appearance with any singer before him would have changed the nature of the occasion. He gloried in raw intensity. His hair was shockingly long and greasy, combed back into what was politely referred to as a ducktail; his curled lip defied the convention that singers must be either smiling or soulful; his body was a frenzy of coital spasms. And of course his voice, gritty, raucous, shrieked and moaned and hiccuped the native woodnotes wild of the rutting season. Uh, "suggestive."

Everybody recognized the symptoms right away, but they hadn't expected to see it in public. It was ominous, shocking, a harbinger of moral chaos. To like him was to take a dare; to imitate him, a defiance that idle young kids, lower-class and white-trash *manqués*, readily adopted. Despised they might be, but Elvis gave them a style of their own on the margin of the mainstream that was forced to come to terms with him.

It is hard to remember his impact now, because he became an institution in record time. He didn't mean to, any more than he meant to rebel. He really was just himself, troubled when people disapproved of him, flattered when they loved him. He loved his mother with touching devotion, he sirred and ma'amed his interviewers; though denounced from pulpits, he crooned an album of down-home hymns like "The Old Rugged Cross"; he served in the Army with dutiful patriotism, refusing special treatment available to him as an entertainer. He unaffectedly made it clear he didn't think he was any better than anyone else — which proved oddly reassuring to people who had been making him sound *worse* than anyone else. By the time he died he was about as redolent of sulphuric rebellion as Bing Crosby.

A Brando could grumble that acting was a trivial occupation in a world full of racism and all that, and threaten to leave it for Higher Things. But such self-conscious perspective on his vocation was beyond Presley. He loved what he did and the adulation he got for it, and if he was a rebel he was a rebel *malgré lui*. He was as naïve as his own music, which, apart from his voice, seemed to consist of a three-string guitar and a cowbell.

Though he never developed, rock did, and by the Sixties it had drawn infusions of sophistication from multitudinous sources without ceasing to be, first and last, a youth culture, with suitable affectations. Stars like Bob Dylan and Mick Jagger knew enough about the "objective situation" to impersonate the alienation Elvis never really knew he represented. Their sound was deliberately ugly. When a friend introduced me to Dylan's music, he had played two songs and part of a third before he realized he had the record on at the wrong speed.

Though Dylan was a convert to rock, he had his biggest influence on the rock world as a contemporary folk singer in the protest vein. And by an odd irony, his conversion to rock involved his abandonment of protest music. "Something's happening and you don't know what it is, do you, Mr. Jones?" sang the adult-baiting early Dylan. The times they were a-changin', and a hard rain was gonna fall, thanks to the masters of war. Elvis wouldn't have known what the hell he was talking about. Then, abruptly, Dylan brought in electric guitars, offending many of his folk-protest constituency, and started singing songs of private, often enigmatic interest, as if to tell the offended they could go folk off. When hipper-than-thou avant-gardes-man Nat Hentoff tried to get him to explicate the radical manifesto latent in his early music, Dylan replied wearily (if disingenuously) that they were just *songs,* that's all, and sighed, "I wonder if Tony Bennett has to go through this."

Well, Elvis never had to go through it: nobody ever suspected his songs of harboring a *Weltanschauung.* But kids had realized that his music was theirs, their parents being estopped by breeding and maturity from admitting its funky attraction. That was its original justification and power. But the ultimate result was not only a rock culture but a rock tradition, within which a kind of reconstruction has taken place, rediscovering and incorporating within its conventions many of the things, artistic and substantive, that rock seemed by its nature to reject. Carly Simon is a great torchy-rock singer, often very funny; and she isn't above poking fun at protest. Gordon Lightfoot and Joni Mitchell, like Dylan, have come out of the folk (or neo-folk) scene, and though their songs include a tithe of liberal pieties, there is none of the amplified nihilism of the Sixties in their music, but rather a soft conservative impetus in the form of private concerns and satisfactions. That's where it all started, though much more crudely, with Elvis. The last thing I heard him sing before his death was a Lightfoot song, "Early Morning Rain." He sang it very sweetly, too.

# Stony Rolls

*October 27, 1989*

I took my daughter to see the Rolling Stones Steel Wheels tour when it hit Washington. She wanted to see it more than I did, even though she hadn't been born the day I first heard "I Can't Get No Satisfaction." As a matter of fact, I've never been a Stones fan. My attitude toward them has mellowed from strong distaste to simple indifference, with a continuing curiosity about their appeal. To me they're the Stony Rolls: hard to get into, not much flavor.

The Stones filled Robert F. Kennedy Stadium both nights they performed. We luckily went the first night, a cool clear evening: a chilly rain drenched the second night. As we filed into the stadium I noticed wryly that the crowd's spirits seemed undepressed by the previous day's news that Irving Berlin had expired. The great majority were no older than my daughter.

You have to give the Stones one thing: they've set a record for protracted trendiness. These kids hadn't been drawn by nostalgia: they like the Stones *right now*. I'd thought of this event as a farewell tour, Mick Jagger being 46 and all, but it's by way of promoting a new album, *Steel Wheels*. It's said to be their best album in several years, by those who can make distinctions I can't.

The opening act, in the twilight, was a black rock band called Living Color. The lead singer, a little guy with dreadlocks that hung to his shoulders, bounced around, his hair flying, trying to occupy a huge stage, more than 250 feet wide, whose full resources were being reserved for the main act. In other circumstances, Living Color would be the featured attraction, but in the fading sunlight, with too much space to fill and most of the crowd inattentive, they looked rather pitiful, desperate.

When they'd finished, there was a long, long hiatus as stagehands rearranged the furnishings and darkness thickened. At several points the crowd stood and roared, thinking the Stones were coming out. The false alarms intensified a tremendous sense of excitement, palpable even to the recusant.

When the Stones finally made their entrance, the roar that went up was the sort of thrilling noise you hear when the home team takes the field for the seventh game of the World Series. The enormous stage was filled with multicolored light from hundreds of bulbs. Jagger plunged into "Start Me Up," the backup instruments amplified at bone-shuddering volume. Your basic rock concert wouldn't be entirely lost on Helen Keller.

Even from relatively choice seats on the field, Jagger was a small, distant figure. The best way to watch him was on one of the three big TV screens overhead. In fact, that was the best way to make sure it was really *him*. He doesn't do anything lots of others couldn't simulate plausibly, from a certain remove.

By now Jagger is simulating himself, as if Elvis had lived on to make a second career as an Elvis impersonator. His bad-boy antics have become conventional, like a professional wrestler's. His motions — snapping head, thrusting arm, skipping across the stage — are the same ones he was doing on *The Ed Sullivan Show* nearly a generation ago. Now as then, he's vocally and physically limited, self-repetitious, self-consciously funky.

Actually, none of the Stones except Keith Richards seems to have any real interest in rock any more. Jagger told one interviewer he can't listen to their early records and doesn't have any favorites among current groups. But he knows the value of a dollar, having attended the London School of Economics once upon a time, so he and Richards overlook their famous differences long enough to do the occasional album, the tour. This year they may gross $100 million. Jagger is really a prudent soul whose longevity is due to bourgeois habits at odds with the rock ethos: he's avoided the usual pitfalls of drug overdoses, crooked managers, marriage to Yoko Ono. Limited though he is, he comes onstage trim and fit, ready to give value for money. He's preserved his demeanor of hard-bitten callowness.

For any reader who may still be unclear about the difference between rock and cabaret singing, the Stones' amplifiers and lights were powered by four generators putting out 2,400,000 watts, enough to sustain forty city blocks. During "Honky-Tonk Woman," two gigantic inflatable honky-tonk women, each 55 feet tall, ballooned on either side of the stage. As countless combinations of colored lights flashed, the sweet odor of marijuana wafted into my nostrils. My daughter traced it to a middle-aged couple in the row in front of us. Like most of the crowd, they were singing along with the more familiar songs, mimicking even Jagger's hand gestures. If anyone in that stadium looked as if they should have been in mourning for Irving Berlin, it was these two.

The rowdiness of Stones fans is legendary, but this was a long way from Altamont. The audience was overwhelmingly young, white, middle-class, and well-behaved. Raucous whoops seemed to be obligatory, but they were the sort of thing you might hear from Lee Atwater after a couple of beers. They peaked when Jagger flirted with one of his backup singers, a pretty black girl dressed up to look like a piece of Harlem harlotry. Maybe I'm jaded, but to me it was about as daring as cutting shop class.

Oh well. Everybody had a good time. That's the important thing.

# Bard Thou Never Wert

*April 29, 1991*

The "William Shakespeare" we know is both fact and artifact, a composition of nineteenth-century scholarship and sentiment. No serious biography of him was undertaken until nearly two hundred years after his death, when Shakespeare studies became a heavy industry, inseparable from Bardolatry.

But the biographers never really caught their man. The portrait that emerged from research was unsatisfying. Maybe it was just the skimpiness of the records, but nothing in the new data reflected a literary life or personality — just a businessman.

Inevitably, skepticism arose. Was Shakespeare even the author of "Shakespeare's" plays? Was he perhaps a front man for the real author? The facts could bear that hypothesis. But then who *was* the real author?

Francis Bacon? That was the most popular alternative to the Stratfordian orthodoxy. But the Baconian theory was tin-eared and cranky. Sensitive skeptics, such as Henry James, Walt Whitman, and Mark Twain, found Bacon and Shakespeare equally unbelievable.

The furious authorship controversy had finally died down by 1920, with the Stratfordians holding the academic high ground, when an English schoolmaster named John Thomas Looney hit upon the most plausible candidate to displace Shakespeare, for those who still cared to: Edward de Vere, 17th Earl of Oxford (1550-1604). More recently, Oxford's case has been upheld by Charlton Ogburn Jr., who has propelled the long-dormant authorship question onto prime-time TV and before a panel of U.S. Supreme Court Justices. Even professional Shakespeareans have begun to treat the issue with a certain respect.

The Oxfordians are still a long way from prevailing, but their fortunes have improved vastly since the nadir of 1943, when their chief spokesman, Percy Allen, went flaky on them in his old age and nearly demolished the cause for all time: he published a book transcribing his conversations with Oxford, Shakespeare, and Bacon at a series of seances. Literati hooted.

At any rate, Shakespeare is the only great author whose claim to his masterpieces has ever been seriously disputed. Nobody who knows the facts of Milton's life, for example, can doubt that he wrote *Paradise Lost.* But Shakespeare is a wraith. His name appears on some early quarto editions of the plays and poems, and the great Folio of 1623 testifies to his authorship. But what if these were deliberate deceptions? The works bearing his name lack the internal evidence of the little personal touches, details, and associations that usually connect an author with his work, whether or not he is conscious of them.

Shakespeare's life, as conventionally told, is full of strange silences at nearly every point when we would expect to hear from him. He never replies to public attacks and needlings. He never acknowledges public praise or reciprocates it. He writes no eulogies for Spenser, Queen Elizabeth, Prince Henry, or other distinguished contemporaries who predecease him. He apparently doesn't complain when his plays are pirated, or even when his name is put on published plays he obviously didn't write. He doesn't write the dedication to his own Sonnets; someone else supplies the prefatory epistle to *Troilus and Cressida.* He vanishes from the London records for eight years after 1604, when he should have been at the height of his fame in the city. No friend, acquaintance, or hanger-on has recorded a single *bon mot*, remark, or opinion from his lips, not even in the First Folio, where he seems to be remembered fondly. (Legends of his roistering with Ben Jonson at the Mermaid arose much later.) Outside his published works, he says nothing; and this taciturnity is strongly at odds with the impression the works themselves leave, of a ready wit and irrepressibly generous eloquence.

Even stranger is London's silence at his death. Only a month earlier, young Francis Beaumont had died, receiving the tribute of verses by his fellow poets and burial in Westminster Abbey. Yet when Shakespeare died in April 1616 *there is not one syllable of recorded reaction.*

Why not? His plays were performed constantly; his name was commercially valuable; seven years later his collected works would be published in a volume of unprecedented opulence, with panegyrics likening him to Aeschylus and Sophocles. If he was known to be the real author of the works bearing his name, it's unthinkable that his death should fail to occasion an outpouring of praise and grief. Instead — no mention.

Conventional scholarship has tried to ignore such puzzles. Shakespeare "biographies" parlay a handful of business and legal records into four-hundred-page guesses, straining to connect the life with the plays and poems. They always founder on the profound inconsistency between the voluble genius we encounter in the works and the tight-lipped burgher we find in the records. The two can't be unified.

And Oxford? A renowned courtier, athlete, poet, playwright, and patron. No plays have survived with his name on them, but Francis Meres (1598) lists him "among the best for comedy," and George Puttenham (1589) tells us Oxford would have been even more famous if he had written under his own name.

Oxford's path crosses "Shakespeare's" in numerous ways. Dozens of incidents in the plays seem to echo incidents in his turbulent life: the Gad's Hill robbery, the Montague-Capulet feud, the stabbing of Polonius, incarcerations in the Tower of London, Timon's bankruptcy, Hamlet's capture by pirates in the Channel, and many others.

As a young man, Oxford visited Europe for over a year, spending much of his time in Venice and other northern Italian cities where so many of the plays are set. This could explain "Shakespeare's" seeming familiarity with actual sites in Venice. The name of Kate the Shrew's father, Baptista Minola, seems to conflate the names of two Italians Oxford did business with, Baptista Nigrone and Pasquino Spinola. Contrary to many a footnote to *The Winter's Tale,* the painter Giulio Romano *was* a sculptor as well; Oxford would be more likely to know this than Shakespeare.

It's common knowledge that "Shakespeare" drew heavily on the classical and Biblical translations of Arthur Golding. As it happens, Golding was the uncle and tutor of the precocious boy Edward de Vere and dedicated a book to him. The great Lord Burghley, Oxford's father-in-law, strikingly resembles Polonius in his inveterate scheming, spying, and garrulous moralizing. The early Sonnets urging the young man to marry are usually thought to have been addressed to the Earl of Southampton; at the probable time of their composition, the early 1590s, Southampton was engaged to Oxford's daughter Elizabeth — a match he backed out of. The Folio is dedicated to the Herbert brothers, the Earls of Pembroke and Montgomery, both close friends of Oxford; Montgomery was Oxford's son-in-law. Oxford also wrote prefaces to two books whose influence is visible in *Hamlet,* Castiglione's *The Courtier* and Thomas Bedingfield's translation of *Cardanus Comfort.* At the very least, there seems to be some mysterious link between Oxford and "Shakespeare."

Consider the Sonnets. Shakespeare biographers have never been able to integrate them convincingly into Shakespeare's life; they never seem to touch the known facts. But they make much more sense as a guarded revelation of Oxford's life. The sonneteer continually refers to his age, lameness, lost friends, and impending death; he jokes that he lies to his mistress about his age. Shakespeare would have been, by conventional dating, about thirty; Oxford was 14 years older. The latest of the Sonnets is usually assigned to 1603, the year before Oxford's death. And why were the Sonnets published (in 1609) with an obscure dedication, not by the poet, but by the publisher, who seems to take it upon himself to dedicate the book on the poet's behalf? And why is the poet referred to as "ever-living" — the sort of phrase you use of a man who is already dead? Shakespeare was 45 and going strong, by all indications; Oxford had been dead for five years. (A 1607 tribute to "Shakespeare," by one William Barkstead, speaks of him in the past tense: "His song was worthy merit." It's also interesting that the so-called "apocryphal" plays bearing Shakespeare's name — *The Puritan*, *The London Prodigal*, and others — began appearing the year after Oxford died.)

The preface to the 1609 quarto of *Troilus and Cressida* is similarly coy and cryptic. The playwright is referred to only as "this author" (though the name "William Shakespeare" appears on the title page), and the reader is advised that "when he is gone, and his comedies out of sale, you will scramble for them" — in other words, buy them now, while you can. Again, why didn't "this author" speak for himself? Why all the mystery about this supposedly active playwright of the public theater? It seems a little presumptuous to speak of a 45-year-old man as soon to be "gone"! (I speak as a 45-year-old man.)

Conventional scholarship has never been able to answer these questions. Assume that "Shakespeare" was really Oxford, though, and it all makes sense: a dead author's identity, perhaps known to the cognoscenti but publicly unmentionable, is being dealt with delicately without being quite acknowledged.

A few difficulties remain:
- *Why should Oxford's identity have to be concealed, even years after his death?* It would have been scandalous for a great lord to be involved in the public theater. The scandal would presumably have disturbed his family (especially his powerful in-laws) more than Oxford himself.
- *Doesn't the date of* The Tempest *(which seems to echo an account of a 1609 shipwreck in Bermuda) rule out Oxford's authorship?* We don't know when *The Tempest* was written; but it could as easily recall a 1595 shipwreck in Bermuda, involving a fleet in which Oxford had once owned an interest.
- *Doesn't Robert Greene's* Groatsworth of Wit (1592) *contain an obvious personal attack on Shakespeare, the "upstart crow"?* The attack certainly alludes to either Shakespeare of Stratford or "Shakespeare" the playwright (whose name never appeared on a published play, by the way, until 1598). But the very obliqueness of the attack should caution us against accepting the simple conventional interpretation. There is a mystery here, as there is everywhere we expect to hear from Shakespeare in his own person.
- *Were Ben Jonson and the others lying in their Folio tributes to Shakespeare?* They were sustaining a necessary fiction. Even at that, much of what they said is evasive or demonstrably untrue. "Shakespeare" is praised only as a writer; we learn next to nothing of him as a man.

**Prick Up Your Ears**

Another order of evidence can be found in Oxford's surviving letters. William Plumer Fowler has made a remarkable compilation of hundreds of parallels of phrase between "Shakespeare" and Oxford. Here is a sampling. In each case, a brief quotation from Oxford's letters is followed, in parentheses, by one or two from "Shakespeare."

1. "It is my hap according to the English proverb to starve like the horse, while the grass doth grow." ("Ay, sir, but while the grass grows — the proverb is something musty.")

2. "To bury and insevill your works in the grave of oblivion." ("And deeper than oblivion do we bury ...")

3. "To bring all my hope in her Majesty's gracious words to smoke." ("This helpless smoke of words." And: "Words folded up in smoke.")

4. "Your news ... doth ring dolefully in the ears of every man." ("Then little strength rings out the doleful knell.")

5. "Decked with pearls and precious stones." ("Decked with diamonds and Indian stones.")

6. "To bury my hopes in the deep abyss and bottom of despair." ("In the dark backward and abysm of time." And: "In the deep bosom of the ocean buried.")

7. "Conceit, which is dangerous." ("Dangerous conceits.")

8. "Thus I leave you to the protection of Almighty God." ("So I leave you to the protection of the prosperous gods.")

9. "In all kindness and kindred." ("A little more than kin, and less than kind.")

10. "In an eternal remembrance to yourself." ("Together with remembrance of ourselves.")

11. "An end according to mine expectation." ("Our expectation hath this day an end.")

12. "By these lewd fellows." ("By this lewd fellow.")

13. "But now time and truth have unmasked all difficulties." ("Time's glory is ... to unmask falsehood and bring truth to light.")

14. "Fruits of golden promises." ("Golden promises." And: "Fruitful ... promises.")

The ear that is intimate with "Shakespeare" may prick up at familiar tricks of phrase, syntax, and metaphor in other Oxfordisms: "Yet am I as one who has long besieged a fort, and not able to compass the end or reap the fruit of his travail ... having passed the pikes of so many adversaries ... knit in alliance ... fair conditioned ... to take advantage of any prosperous gale, or with anchor to ride till the storm be overpast ... most earnestly to crave both your opinion and counsel ... their nearer consanguinity ... perverse and impudent dealing ... inclined and affected to me ... employed for the better achieving ... to bear and support them with patience ... salve so great an inconvenience ... the best expectation of my tedious suit ... to illuster yourself with the ornaments of virtue ... otherwise affaired with the business of the commonwealth ... intercepted by these unlooked-for troubles ... being thus disfurnished and unprovided ..."

Even so short a list offers telling and distinctive subtleties: the ready imagery (often military or maritime), the free coinages, the interchanging of parts of speech, the fondness for the gerund, the exuberant redundancies, the moral themes and attitudes, the rhythms, the intensifiers, the energetic variety, the sheer authority of expression. This isn't the voice of Spenser, or Marlowe, or Jonson, or Generic Elizabethan. It's the voice of "Shakespeare."

All this is likely to be very upsetting to anyone who cherishes Shakespeare. For to love Shakespeare is to have formed a certain mental image of the author: the genius of modest origins, the man of Stratford whose second-best bed is as much a part of his lore as "Friends, Romans, countrymen" — a dear democratic myth, really. And to be told that "he" was really some nobleman — one of the "wolfish earls," as Whitman shrewdly suspected, the spirit of whose works is "non-acceptable to democracy" — well, really! But there it is, confirmed from every angle.

How is it, we may ask, that the elusively omniscient genius of classroom legend, this nobody/Everyman of allegedly "universal sympathies," should view life so constantly from the angle of the ruling class of his day? If he's the Stratfordian commoner, it's certainly odd that nearly all his common characters are one-dimensional buffoons, viewed with kindly humor but no deep interest. His kings and lords, on the other hand, are highly individuated.

**No Traitor to His Class**

If we see things aright, we realize that Oxford subtly reveals himself in these plays by assuming the perspective of his class. After all, you tend to see members of your own class as individuals, and those of other classes primarily as types. Those Marxist critics who accuse Shakespeare of being a reactionary bourgeois don't know the half of it. The real "Shakespeare" displays an unwaveringly feudal conservatism that makes Russell Kirk look like Robespierre. If the common people amuse him as individuals, they horrify him as a mob. But by no means does he hate them; he simply doesn't feel that strongly about them.

Consider Dogberry, the officious, malaprop-prone magistrate who blunderingly catches the villains in *Much Ado*.

Oxford-"Shakespeare" views this fool indulgently, as a harmless prop of social order. Contrast Mr. Bumble — exactly the same social type, except that Dickens hates him. The difference is that Dickens had been at his mercy, and knew what a maddening petty tyrant he could be; an experience Oxford's high birth had spared him.

For some reason, Oxford seems to have withdrawn from Elizabeth's court, where he had known both glory and disgrace, and spent his later years happily slumming in the popular theater. His plays are full of lords who leave the court, either to adopt a simpler life or to assume humble disguises. And it was in the theater that Oxford obscured his own lordship, and achieved his majesty.

# Less Is More

*May 11, 1979*

NBC has rebroadcast Franco Zefirelli's *Jesus of Nazareth*, and its very excellences point up its failure. Nearly everything about it is fine; I don't expect ever to see a better version of the Gospel story; but somehow it doesn't work.

Part of the problem is that it's one of those Who's Who spectaculars: a synod of great actors in great cameos — Ustinov, Plummer, Olivier, Richardson, Mason. Ustinov, as Herod, is a terrifying figure, all right, not because of any royal grandeur but precisely because he embodies pure petulance liberated by absolute power, raging with violent self pity at the rumor of a *baby*. But then he's gone, and it's somebody else's turn to be memorable for a minute. By the time Ernest Borgnine and Anthony Quinn turn up, it's wearing pretty thin. The big names flashing by have the unfortunate effect of emphasizing the discontinuity of the Gospels, especially when they are conflated to get all the facts in. The acting, the dusty visual beauty, the pungent Jewishness of the intimate scenes — these are undermined by the attempt to be comprehensive.

It seems cruel to dispraise Robert Powell's Jesus, a noble and tasteful effort, neither saccharine nor sanctimonious; but avoiding vice isn't the same thing as achieving virtue. Often he is lovable, always he is inoffensive — which is the trouble. Jesus went around shocking as he healed, performing miracles to stave off enemies for a while, withholding claims more shocking than the ones he made publicly. And even his confidants were shocked by his confidences. Powell gives us a Jesus who is too easily taken for granted, a conventional Jesus. He should have reminded us how strange the convention itself is. As lawyers say, one needs a certain "standing" to forgive sins — you must be either the victim of particular sins, or else God. A man who without explanation tells people that their sins are forgiven is on the face of it annoying, at least. The saner he seems, the more outrageous. Nobody but a villain could feel the urge to humiliate and kill a nice British gentleman like Powell's Jesus. But we shouldn't be permitted to feel so superior to those who hated Christ; and this production lets us feel superior even to the disciples.

Of course we have an unfair advantage over them to begin with: we know how the story comes out. But that very fact turns the story into ritual, whereas the point of a dramatization is to dramatize, to immerse our emotions in the flow of events. Jesus has to be made more vivid than an icon, and we must at least be made to feel why people no worse than most of us could marvel, wonder, be troubled and antagonized by him. We aren't innocent enough to react that way to this story; for us the Good News is stale news. The dramatist must help us to approach it freshly, like a little child. Anthony Burgess' script spares us the rod and spoils us with grown-up familiarity.

Burgess himself is a lapsed Catholic, he says, and this has one good effect: he left his faith at once rather than by the liberalizing degrees that so often reduce the Gospels to a de-supernaturalized husk before they are finally discarded; so, while treating it as a fiction, he allows the story its integrity. But this also causes him to tell it with a nostalgic reverence that ignores its urgency, its challenge, its danger to those who hear it. So he avoids inventing dialogue for Jesus, and Powell must speak like a walking Bartlett's, while those around him are free to talk politics and weather and ask where the men's room is.

In this solemn isolation the invented contexts are too artificial, the Word lacks flesh, and his give-and-take with the word becomes pure sermon *cum*-soulful-gazing rather than mutual provocation. To be flesh is to be commonplace and therefore to have frequent occasion to say less than eloquent things; the real challenge of portraying Jesus is to show him between his miracles of act and word. If we can see him eating, we should be able to hear him asking for the butter and commenting on the food. Otherwise his great utterances can't surprise and we know that every time Powell opens his mouth we are about to hear something we already know. The Gospels do not present a Jesus of aloofness and taciturnity; they are deliberately concentrated and stylized, but their Jesus is a *presence* which Powell must attempt futilely to convey, in between the red-letter speeches, with looks of pensive kindliness. What we want is fiery love, and this is falsified by reverent silences.

Can that presence possibly be conveyed? Perhaps it must be done obliquely if at all. C.S. Lewis tried through the medium of fairy tales. As he once explained: "Why did one find it so hard to feel as one ought to feel about God or about the sufferings of Christ? I thought the chief reason was that one was told one ought to. An obligation to feel can freeze feelings. And reverence itself did harm. The whole subject was associated with lowered voices: almost as if it were something medical. But supposing that by casting all these things into an imaginary world, stripping them of their stained-glass and Sunday School associations, one could make them for the first time appear in their real potency? Could one not thus steal past those watchful dragons? I thought one could."

So Lewis invented the kingdom of Narnia and the lion Aslan, a Christ-like (though not, so to speak, Powell-like) figure to whom he could give invented words without fear of sacrilege. Aslan is less Christ than an imaginative equivalent, a brilliant and successful intimation of here-and-now holiness, like first love's joys and fears re-created.

The Children's Television Workshop has produced a fine animated version of the first of the Narnia tales, *The Lion, the Witch and the Wardrobe*. CBS showed it in two hour-long segments, the first of which overlapped with the first night of *Jesus of Nazareth*. No doubt it will be shown again; and I hope the Workshop will exercise its right to produce the whole Narnia cycle. Apart from its general wit and fancy, this *Lion*'s suggestive analogies conveyed far more of Gethsemane and Calvary than *Jesus'* literal version. Who would think a cartoon of a dead lion could top Olivier & Co.? But it did, precisely because it chose imagination over pious associations. As they say, less is more. Maybe that's a Gospel lesson.

# The Lord and the Bard

*August 18, 1989*

By the time he died, the younger English actors were saying his acting style was "calculated," mechanical, essentially heartless. It was a style he had invented and perfected and taken beyond all previous ideas of perfection. They might as well denigrate it; there was no hope at all of rivaling him at it.

The chorus of detractors included Olivier himself. "Tricks, my dear fellow," he told a *Newsweek* interviewer who had asked for the secrets of his art. "Don't you realize they're nothing more than tricks?"

But that may have been Olivier playing his longest-running role, World's Greatest Actor, luxuriating in modesty on a scale only he could afford. After (say) 1964, the year of his Othello, not even he could diminish his stature.

He loved to talk about those "tricks," a thousand of which will remain observable forever, in dozens of filmed performances that will suffice to explain his reputation to future generations. The common principle behind them all is surprise. *Never do what the audience expects*. This underlies the famous sudden rages, the equally sudden flashes of wit, the subtle pauses, the hints of effeminacy that complicated his bounding virility.

"Young man," an older actress once told him, "you are a gorgeous creature on stage, but you are altogether too predictable in what you do." For instance, she said, you should pause for breath in the middle of sentences, not at the end. That was the difference between acting and declaiming. "Audiences love to be surprised, to be shocked." He only had to be told once. He would outrage critics, but none of them ever thought to damn him with that single fatal word: "predictable." When his Titus Andronicus received word that his sons had been killed (after he'd allowed his own hand to be chopped off as ransom), he leaned back and laughed softly. How the next Titus played the scene is not recorded.

Electrifying audiences was his trade. He discussed acting, in books and interviews, almost as if it were crowd control. In the great Shakespearean roles, make a quiet opening entrance. Let the audience see you on a human scale first, so they can sympathize with you; save the roaring for later. "If you have succeeded in the initial moments, either by a very strong stamp of characterization so they recognize you as a real guy, or by a quiet approach, then I think there's no end to where you can lead them in size of acting a little later in the evening."

And when your Othello or Lear does roar, he said, you must never quite hit the top of your voice. Always keep something in reserve, never show the audience your limits. You have to seem potentially infinite.

Olivier's preoccupation with externals was notorious: false noses, dyed hair, a rainbow of greasepaints. He derided Method acting. Most of his inspiration went into preparation, conceiving roles anew and then revising every physical detail. All this gave him something solid to fall back on in case of an opening-night adrenaline shortage, which rarely happened. During his Oedipus and Titus, some spectators had to be carried out; medical teams stood by to succor overwrought nervous systems. Such is the magic of great acting, aided by gouged eyeballs and severed hands.

Terror and pity, says Aristotle, are the chemistry of tragedy. Olivier was better at the terror part. He understood audiences; he didn't really understand Shakespeare, except as a mother-lode of great opportunities for stardom. His education was on the boards, not in the study. Two of his greatest successes came in two of Shakespeare's hammiest roles, Titus and Richard III.

Olivier's Richard (filmed and now on a cheap video) is enhanced by the splendid gimmickry of his technique. But the actor's defects show up in his moody, Freudian Hamlet (also on video) and his Othello and Lear (not yet available). These are not only great roles but also, of course, pinnacles of the poetic imagination. For them, trickery won't do.

Olivier played Hamlet under the tutelage of Ernest Jones, Freud's chief English exponent, who planted in Olivier's bleached head the notion that Hamlet was afflicted with an Oedipus complex, and was thus "a man who could not make up his mind." (You know the type.) This theory explains nothing about the play but does account for the film's interlinear obsession with beds and mother-son smooching — still mildly daring stuff in the Forties.

For Othello, Olivier turned to F.R. Leavis' crabby essay debunking the assumption that the hero is, as his final speech says, "not easily jealous." The essay might do as a courtroom plea by Iago's defense attorney, but it flattens the whole play. Not that Olivier minded: it enabled him to turn the greatest duel in drama into a one-man show. Iago was reduced to a surly prop, hardly necessary to ignite such an emotional self-starter as this volatile Moor (who seemed suspiciously Jamaican). It didn't help matters that Maggie Smith's Desdemona totally lacked the ethereal innocence that can lift a man's heart to adoration; she was a sturdy English girl who seemed perfectly capable of taking care of herself. It wouldn't have made much difference to this version of the play if she *had* been carrying on with Cassio. Olivier enacted raw jealousy — the wounded male ego in full fury — as nobody else ever will, with full measure of histrionic *frisson.* What he missed was "the pity of it, Iago" — the grief, deeper than any rage, of the man who has glimpsed heaven and lost it.

As always, Olivier had found a novel theatrical angle for his interpretation. He told Kenneth Tynan that "I'm sure Shakespeare meant there to be a great splash of sexual shock" in the interracial union of Othello and Desdemona. So he'd heightened the swaggering negritude, in defiance of the text (which stresses Othello's reserve) but in tune with 1964's topicalities. It never crossed his mind that Shakespeare might have had a purpose beyond wowing 'em. Shocks, thrills, surprises, emotional danger: this was Olivier's art. There's more to Shakespeare's.

His 1983 Lear, made for TV, had his usual physical authority, only slightly diminished by old age. No matter how wrongheadedly he played a Shakespearean role, he fixed his own ineffaceably magnificent image of it in your mind. But this time the quiet opening didn't serve him well. After all, we meet Lear on his worst behavior; as someone has said, Shakespeare doesn't ask our sympathy for him on easy terms. Lear is the consummate tragic hero, whose stubborn will precipitates a terrible fate; he may not deserve it, but he asks for it. Lear is not a victim of circumstance, and in his self-inflicted helplessness he must undergo a tremendous conversion. Olivier's Lear was so ingratiating (and rather weak) in the first scene that there wasn't much call for either his suffering or his change of heart. It was sad, not tragic; not even very moving.

The question is not at all whether Olivier was a great actor, but whether he reached the very highest peaks. To say that he never quite made it is not to belittle what he did achieve. The thrills were genuine, more than the sum of "tricks." (In a way, Archie Rice was Olivier's nightmare, the performer whose tricks all fizzled miserably before empty, silent houses.) As James Agee observed, no actor since Chaplin was so complete a master of all that the body can contribute to a role. Olivier could speak a line of Shakespeare as if it had just occurred to him; his unique rhythm and energy are as evident in the *pianissimo* passages as in the Agincourt ripsnorters. He was not only versatile but versatile at a magnitude few actors achieve even once. Being gigantic was the only trick he never managed to explain.

# The Feast of St. Gilbert

*September 14, 1979*

"Thy life's a miracle," Shakespeare's Edgar tells his despairing father. The line might serve as G.K. Chesterton's credo. Earlier this year I went to Toronto for a meeting of the Chesterton Society, presided over by Father Ian Boyd, who also edits *The Chesterton Review*. The meeting itself was a bit of a miracle.

People came from as far off as Alberta and England. One of the speakers was Russell Kirk. In the audience sitting a row ahead of me at one point was another familiar-looking figure whom I couldn't place. The tiny tape recorder he held up to record the speech should have jostled the right association; but I didn't realize who he was until another speaker nodded politely to him and spoke of "Professor McLuhan." Kirk and McLuhan aren't usually spoken of in the same breath, but in Chesterton they are united.

Chesterton today is less known than known about. He used to be known as the forelegs of the Chesterbelloc, Bernard Shaw's comic beast, defender of the Catholic faith. The Church he championed has been assumed, since Vatican II, to be under new management. He is also known as the creator of Father Brown, one of those quaint English detectives who proliferated in the Age of Holmes. More recently he has been held in suspicion as an antisemite, though his marginal criticisms of Jews were not unmixed with sympathy. (He never confused fault-finding with hurting, and he lashed out at Hitler very early.)

Worst of all, he is assumed to be merely quaint. He crusaded not only for Catholicism but for *Distributivism*, which some mistake for a mere medieval restoration. It was not that; as Father Boyd points out in his brilliant book on Chesterton's fictions, he thought it was dangerous folly to try to bring the Middle Ages back. (He was, after all, an ardent admirer of the French Revolution.) But he thought the medieval form of propertied liberty was valuable as an ordering ideal. Genuine ideals are timeless, and Chesterton was without a trace of what C.S. Lewis called "chronological snobbery."

He had no other snobbery in him either. He wrote for all occasions, however trifling, with generous humor, in the ephemeral form of the newspaper essay and the old-fashioned forms of allegory, light fiction, and rhymed stanzas. All evidence suggests that he had little care for his literary reputation. His enthusiasms were almost embarrassingly promiscuous, high and low together, like My Last Duchess' smiles: Shakespeare and Conan Doyle, Blake and Dickens, Henry James and R.L. Stevenson. Nor did he segregate categories according to the modern custom: all his concerns, personal, political, religious, are buoyantly present in his literary criticism. He was the most topical of geniuses.

But for that reason the task of reconstructing his milieu is enormous. Only a few of his books remain in print, and gathering his journalistic writings and letters is a feat for Hercules. Unfashionable enough in his own day, he dwelt among people even more eccentric and certainly crankier than himself, an enclave against modernity. The Chesterton Society, largely through the *Review,* is piecing the picture together. Despite some inevitable pedantry, it is on the whole a refreshing enterprise.

It is a commonplace that history is written by the victors. Most modern people have taken a progressive view for the simple and unconscious reason that the historical process, for all its faults, has culminated in themselves. Chesterton was shrewd enough to see the narrowness of such progressivism, and through hindsight we can see it too. It is easy, of course, to feel smugly superior to a man who felt transitory approval for Mussolini; even if we might better consider how Mussolini must have looked in 1930, if so humane a man as Chesterton could approve of him. What is more startling is that Chesterton, who inveighed against the "science" of eugenics (soon to become an applied science), foresaw its disastrous consequences. In this, writes Margaret Canovan, Chesterton stood outside the mainstream of what then passed for enlightened liberalism. (Oliver Wendell Holmes supported mandatory sterilization, Harry Jaffa reminds me.) His defense of the poor was rooted in a defense of the family and of liberty against those state planners who pined for population refinement. It is not hard to see the likeness to those enlightened souls who think the state should now promote contraception and abortion among the poor. Once you understand his *topoi*, Chesterton's topicality turns out to have surprising pertinence. *The Chesterton Review* is thus keeping alive what has become a fugitive tradition of social criticism. It reminds us that we who are alive today are the lucky survivors of Nazism and related evils; those of the next generation will be the lucky survivors of abortion "reform."

Impossible to pin down, Chesterton is a living challenge to today's reader as perhaps no other author of his time can still be. He drives out complacent urbanity with his own strange power, a kind of divine urbanity. He dares you to love life with a zest like his; and it is a supremely friendly dare.

At the meeting we got an unexpected taste of his presence. Father Boyd had two short tapes of Chesterton speaking publicly, shortly before his death in 1936. His voice was very British, with a halting and diffident joviality that was utterly disarming. "… In the confusion of the moment, I was taken for a man of letters." We laughed with the taped audience, in a transgenerational unanimity of mirth. "My first thought was to explain that I was not a man of letters, but a mere lecturer. But that would not do, for there were some present who had heard me lecture." More laughter across time. And more, for twenty sweet minutes.

When the tape finally ended, it was as if the room were not only quieter but darker, and emptier.

# Olivier

*October 25, 1974*

When several of Laurence Olivier's Shakespeare films came back to New York recently, it occurred to me that he has not performed a Shakespearean role in this country for nearly a quarter of a century. The last one was Antony in 1951, to his then-wife Vivien Leigh's Cleopatra. The only previous one was Romeo, to Leigh's Juliet, in 1940. His Shakespearean reputation here rests largely on his films: *Henry V, Hamlet, Richard III,* and *Othello.* So handsome are they, and so electrifying is Olivier's reading of their verse, that no adverse critical estimate of them should deter him who hasn't seen them.

But. These same films also embody the much that is wrong with Olivier's Shakespearean conceptions, and with Shakespearean productions in general. Apropos of the theatrical gimmickry so often inflicted on the poet, *Time*'s T.E. Kalem has remarked that it all suggests a fear that the greatest playwright who ever lived can't be counted on to hold an audience without "help." Directors live in deathly fear of being thought stodgy, and I have heard of a production of *A Midsummer Night's Dream* in which all the males had light bulbs in their codpieces, which lit up at moments of amorousness.

Olivier's tampering is of a different order. The first of his Shakespeare films, *Henry V,* a wartime film he himself produced to build English morale, may be forgiven for scanting Henry's bloody egotism — not that Olivier would have noticed it anyway. His Richard III is widely regarded as one of his greatest roles; though some complained that he made Richard a cackling buffoon, his humor pays off in the cobra-like danger it conveys when it snaps off. But Henry and Richard are not really great Shakespearean heroes. Hamlet and Othello are. And the difference is not so much in the stature of the heroes themselves as in the texture of the plays they inhabit. *Richard III* is all theatrical flourish, and can bear a little toying; but cutting a speech from *Hamlet* can be like removing the oboe part from a Mozart symphony. The great roles are traps for actors precisely because they are more than mere "vehicles."

Olivier based his production of *Hamlet* on the theory of psychoanalyst Ernest Jones that Hamlet's problem is an Oedipus complex. One of the many problems with such a simplifying interpretation is that it makes so much of the play irrelevant. If Hamlet only yearns to possess his mother, what in hell has Fortinbras got to do with the price of butter in Denmark? Let alone speeches about what's Hecuba to him, or he to Hecuba, or how in the corrupted currents of this world, offense's gilded hand may shove by justice. And all that stuff was either cut, or nudged into the background while the camera showed where the *real* action was: Hamlet and Gertrude nuzzling, while Claudius, audible but hardly noticeable, was talking poetry; the royal bed of Denmark, solemnly zoomed in on by the camera, while William Walton's music, like a concerto for eight pairs of cymbals, conveyed the gravity of the matter; etc.

*Othello* was filmed, but it wasn't really a film. The idea was simply to make Olivier's stage performance available around the world. Good. But the passivity of the camera was not much help, since Olivier the actor distorted the play singlehandedly by doing it Professor Leavis' way: not the noble Moor, but the jealous Moor, the vain warrior with the built-in Iago. Olivier explained in interviews that he thought the "old" Othello (i.e., Shakespeare's) would appear insufferably gullible to a modern audience. The upshot was to impart a heavy sarcasm to Othello's most innocent words. The night brawl on Cyprus, ingeniously ignited by Iago, became a transparent prank, so that "I know, Iago, thy honesty and love doth mince this matter, making it light to Cassio," sounded like "I know you're lying, you bastard, but I can't prove it."

In the Thirties, Olivier played Iago as a homosexual infatuated with Othello (Ernest Jones again). In 1959, he played Coriolanus' death scene *à la* Mussolini, hanging upside down. And last year ABC presented his Shylock, which was, as you might expect, the bleeding-heart Shylock: still, it was powerfully and plausibly done — until his final exit. Then he cut loose, off-stage, with a howl of grief that interrupted — well, Shakespeare. It was just a dirty lowdown trick on the text.

Sometimes one hears rumbles that he plans to do Lear again, for the first time since 1947. I hope he does. I hope he films it. And most of all, I hope he doesn't read anything that Freud or Jan Kott or Leslie Fiedler may have written on the subject. Let him give one of his straightforward, trumpet-tongued performances; and his sins will be forgiven. As if they wouldn't be anyway.

# A Fair Shake for Oxford

*November 6, 1987*

A thousand people crammed the United Methodist Church across the street from American University in Washington on September 25 to witness a debate on the Shakespeare authorship question. TV crews covered the event, which made the front page of the *New York Times* the next morning. It had been ably promoted by David Lloyd Kreeger, a high-powered Washington businessman and patron of the arts who is convinced that "William Shakespeare" was the pen name of Edward de Vere, 17th Earl of Oxford.

Did I say high-powered? Kreeger managed to get three Supreme Court Justices to adjudicate the debate: William Brennan, Harry Blackmun, and John Paul Stevens. All three ruled in favor of the traditional claimant, but the event lifted the Oxfordian theory out of the crank category. Blackmun and Stevens conceded that the case for Oxford is hard to dismiss, and Brennan, asked whether it was a tough case, smiled, "This was an absolutely impossible one!"

Lawyers for Oxford and William "Shakspere" (as the name was usually spelled in Stratford) each had 45 minutes to present their arguments, plus 15 minutes for rebuttal. The three judges took a long lunch break to deliberate, then returned separate opinions and explained their reasons.

Oxfordians, including me, were disappointed in their lawyer, Peter Jaszi, who spent more time tearing down "Shakspere" than making the positive case for de Vere. In fairness, be it said that Jaszi had a double burden: he had to refute the traditional belief *and* prove Oxford's authorship. Moreover, he had to meet the standard of "clear and convincing evidence ... beyond a reasonable doubt." That's a tall order for an hour's debate: annihilating and supplanting a cherished cultural myth. The very idea that "Shakspere" and "Shakespeare" may have been two different men sounds like a paradox or a quibble to most people.

The debate itself sounded less like a literary dispute than a divorce case, with the two lawyers competing in character assassination of each other's clients. Jaszi argued that Shakspere was an illiterate bumpkin, while James Boyle called Oxford a profligate aristocrat.

As Boyle recounted Oxford's amours, feuds, drinking, and debts, Stevens broke in: "That certainly *sounds* like a playwright."

Whoever wrote the plays, they abound in apparent echoes of incidents in Oxford's turbulent life. Even on the Stratfordian hypothesis it's likely that the two men knew each other: Oxford was a playwright and patron of the theater, at a time when London proper had a population of only 75,000 or so.

But there is bad blood between the orthodox Stratfordians and the heretical Oxfordians. The Stratfordian establishment resists taking up any Oxfordian lead, even though hard information about their own man is scarce. And a leading Oxfordian refused to shake hands when introduced to a top Stratfordian scholar who had insulted his parents (also leading Oxfordians in their day) many years earlier.

The day after the debate, the Shakespeare Oxford Society held its annual meeting in a Washington hotel room. Thanks to the special event and its publicity, attendance was relatively high this year: the room was full. (With fewer than a hundred members nationwide, the Society doesn't yet threaten to become a mass movement.)

The members' feelings about the debate were mixed. Charlton Ogburn Jr., author of the excellent 1984 tome *The Mysterious William Shakespeare*, was inconsolable. A courtly but scrappy Southerner, Ogburn had been pushing for a formal trial of the Oxford thesis for years, and as far as he was concerned it had misfired. But others took the brighter view that the whole affair had been an immense boost for the cause of de Vere. An actual victory, after all, would have been improbable.

So the Oxfordians press on. At my side is a new book, *Shakespeare Revealed in Oxford's Letters*, by William Plumer Fowler (available for $37.50 ppd. from Peter E. Randall Publisher, P.O. Box 4726, Portsmouth, New Hampshire 03801). It's 872 pages long — middling for an Oxfordian book — and it traces verbal parallels between the Earl and "Shakespeare." I've only had time to sample it, but my early impression is that it strengthens Oxford's claim. I recommend it as indispensable to anyone who takes a serious interest in the authorship question — but not without reservations.

If anything, Fowler finds too many parallels between Oxford's turns of phrase in 37 surviving letters and Shakespeare's. "I perceive" and "for fear of" occur often in both bodies of writing, but they are hardly idiosyncratic enough to prove the two authors one.

It's true that the frequency with which a man uses a common idiom can become a sort of personal signature, and this sort of thing is not totally worthless as evidence, but such items don't justify the tone of triumphant confirmation Fowler tends to accord each one separately.

In order to judge, we'd have to know how often the same idioms were used by other Elizabethan writers. Even the more self-consciously figurative language Oxford shares with Shakespeare doesn't prove as much as Fowler would like it to, since many rhetorical and poetic figures that arrest a modern eye turn out to have been conventional in 1600.

But though their separate value may be nil, Fowler's examples do have a cumulative power. After a thousand minor coincidences, it's hard to lay the resemblances to accident. And the similarity transcends enumeration. Eventually one says, with Gloucester in *King Lear,* "The trick of that voice I do well remember." Even the Protean Shakespeare has a distinctive basic manner, and the ear catches it in Oxford.

In one letter he speaks of "bury[ing] my hopes in the deep abyss and bottom of despair." Curiously, Fowler doesn't twig to two Shakespearean echoes. In *Richard III* we find "in the deep bosom of the ocean buried." In *The Tempest*, "in the dark backward and abysm of time."

Another letter complains: "And I am to content myself according to the English proverb that it is my hap to starve like the horse, while the grass doth grow." The proverb said: "While the grass groweth the steed starveth." Compare Hamlet's "Ay, sir, but 'While the grass grows' — the proverb is something musty."

Some of these letters are casual — Elizabethan phone calls. They don't display rampant genius, any more than Joyce's letters do, but they aren't just anyone's letters, either. Throw out the weak specimens, and Fowler still has hundreds to suggest that in Oxford's correspondence we find Shakespeare offstage — a brilliant man at ease, tossing off words and images he'll later knead into astounding concentrated eloquence.

# Priest Bites Bishop

review of
*Catholicism and Modernity: Confrontation or Capitulation?*
(New York, NY: Seabury Press, 1979, 250 pp.) by James Hitchcock

*August 31, 1979*

After reading James Hitchcock's *Catholicism and Modernity: Confrontation or Capitulation?* I am tempted to paraphrase Will Rogers, and say: "I don't belong to any organized religion. I'm a Catholic."

Depressing, yes, in a way. But what an utterly brilliant book this is. Its eye for detail is so sharp, its analysis so profound, that the reader feels the exhilaration of possessing a supreme intellectual vantage over the scene. Never mind that the scene is now gloomy. The book gives the key to restoration.

A sketch will have to do. There is just too much book here, and every page seems to offer new insights, bursting forth like successive explosions of fireworks from preceding insights. Everything connects.

Hitchcock argues that the present disarray of the Catholic Church results from the derailment of renewal. Few people have really understood what went on at the Second Vatican Council. It was the Council's misfortune to have occurred during the giddy Sixties, and to have been confused with a number of contemporary trends. In fact the substance of the Council has usually been ignored, the whole affair being treated instead as a sort of Happening (remember Happenings?), and thereby distorted — deliberately. What we hear about is not so much what the Council did, as what the liberals (Catholic and otherwise) thought it promised. When the alleged promises were not fulfilled, of course, Church authorities were treated as betrayers of the Council. In short, we have been victimized by what might be called the Whig interpreters of the Council.

Put otherwise, the real Council was fully continuous with Catholic tradition. The liberal myth is that it was at least the beginning of a break with that tradition. And ever since, liberal Catholics (or perhaps Catholic liberals would be more exact: the kind who are more liberal than Catholic) have been demanding that the Church get on with its mission of assimilating — or, as Hitchcock would say, capitulating — to modernity.

Of course much depends on what is meant by modernity. The Church has been modernizing in ways consonant with her traditional identity; but if Catholicism means anything distinctive — if, say, the Church speaks, with full apostolic authority, for Jesus Christ — then there have to be limits. Some of her modes can and must be modern, but not her essence. That must be eternal.

Hitchcock begins by discussing the "flight from eternity." The middle-brow intellectuals who set the tone for the Catholic Church in America have edged uncomfortably away from affirmations of transcendence, ignoring and even deriding old-fashioned symbols of the sacred. Such symbols have been attacked as culture-bound, and, following liberal Protestant models, the attackers have sought to purify the Church of its corrupt accretions, returning to the primitive Church of the New Testament.

The problem, of course, is that you can't go home again. If today's Church is distinctive only for her departure from the primitive Church, she is a fraud. But what the liberals call corruption is what Newman called development. And the great irony, as Hitchcock shrewdly observes, is that the "primitive Church" of the liberals strikingly (and conveniently) mirrors the agenda of modern liberalism. Miracle, sacrament, consecrated chastity are all vigorously debunked; they have been replaced by therapy, self-fulfillment, relevance. All traditional disciplines irksome to modern liberalism are ascribed to medieval distortions of the sunny Gospel message. And, now, "nuns seek to become priests, priests get married, and married people get divorced in ever greater numbers."

Catholic liberals thus enjoy a double "sensation of movement": they feel they are moving backward and forward at the same time. What's more, they can do all this while standing still: "Like most apostles of change, avant-garde Catholics oscillate between proclamations of a radically transformed world which will scarcely resemble anything known in the past, and condescending assurances that nothing essential has changed and that traditionalists are merely neurotically insecure."

Hitchcock is at his best when he inspects the dynamics and mechanics of change. Despite all the talk about the "democratization" of the Church, the real ferment is not among the folks in the pews but among the clergy, theologians, intellectuals, and the large and enlarging body of professionals who administer liturgical and catechetical matters at the national and diocesan levels. All these have come to have a vested interest in change. They are the Church's "New Class" (a term Hitchcock wisely avoids, but it won't down), representing its version of the managerial revolution. (Here one might note the similarity between these phenomena and the growing power of academics as a class against the nominal authority of those who preside over the universities — a change whose slogan has been "academic freedom." When a young Yale graduate analyzed the process in 1951, his subjects hotly denied that any such process was proceeding.)

Hitchcock is at his *best* best when he analyzes the way the mass media, our cognitive bureau of standards, have assisted the Catholic New Class. Despite their avowed "pluralism," the media tend to homogenize. They can't assimilate the supernatural, and they exert powerful pressures on all truly distinctive cognitive minorities to submit to their own definitions of reality. Rebels within the Church become the heroes in the media's accounts of events; traditionalists are at best isolated, at worst caricatured and slandered. Defectors from traditional Catholicism can now win publicity and worldly approval while retaining formal membership. In fact they stand to gain more by staying in the Church, however tenuously: priest-bites-bishop is even better copy than man-bites-dog.

Since their real social and psychic solidarity is with the liberal secular world rather than with orthodox believers, members of the Catholic New Class conceive themselves not as bearers of Christ's message to unbelievers, but as the world's missionaries to the Church. Toward the world they tend to be uncritically loyal, Uncle Toms as it were. On the margin there are such types as Jimmy Breslin, "a new kind of stage Irishman … an individual whose claim to attention derives almost entirely from his group identity but who makes his living undermining his group's values at the behest of the dominant elite." The media can't be accused of anti-Catholicism for "merely reporting" what certain selected members of the Church say about her. And when the Berrigans and Cogleys step forth to deliver their "witness," the labors of a Paul Blanshard become otiose.

The inevitable terminus is radical politics. As loyalties are transferred from the supernatural to the world, hope moves from eternity to the future — at least the future as conceived by modernity — at least modernity as conceived by self-conscious Catholics. Which, very often, means variants of Marxism, future-hope *par excellence.* (What is left of the religious impulse takes the form of what Hitchcock shrewdly identifies as spiritual hedonism: only an avant-garde Catholic could, at this late date, look *up* to Harvey Cox.) Hitchcock's devastating accumulation of liberal Catholic fads suggests that the breaking of old taboos in itself offers "self-fulfillment": what moves many Catholics of this type is an insatiable need to validate their "authentic" selves by endless histrionic repudiations of traditional prescriptions, rather than any positive, orienting alternative ideal. The more they reject the Church, the more they feel they have achieved solidarity with the "modern world" of their naughty dreams. That is why many who complain bitterly of the Church's authoritarianism wind up blindly approving of Marxist totalitarianism (if the phrase is not redundant) in China and Vietnam. Their own taboos include anti-Communism; the persecution of the Church in Communist countries is liberal Catholicism's "dirty little secret."

In *Suicide of the West,* James Burnham identifies liberalism not as an autonomous position but as a psycho-social reaction, which tacitly denies that the West contains any core of value worth defending against its enemies. In fact it resists admitting that the enemies *are* enemies. It favors a piecemeal accommodation with them, simultaneously justifying their aggressions and rationalizing Western surrenders. Every Western defeat is interpreted as a victory for "genuine" Western ideals (self-determination, say), and hostility is reserved for those who insist on the reality of conflict and the possibility that something terribly precious is being lost. The hatred of the deluded turns with automatic bitterness on those who challenge the delusion.

Liberal Catholics (I mean Catholic liberals) likewise insist that there is no real conflict between the Church and the world-in-becoming, except of course such conflict as is of the "old" Church's making. Hitchcock, like Burnham, has stunningly laid bare both the impulses behind this mentality and the crasser means and motives that give it force in the real world, all the while exposing its semantic evasions with a kind of satiric objectivity. As he points out, it is "modern" Catholics, not the orthodox, who have sold out to the world, materially and spiritually, internalizing the contempt of their "cultured despisers." It is they, not the orthodox, who are in that sense culture-bound, beholden to the vagaries of the historical moment. *Catholicism and Modernity* richly earns the hatred of the deluded.

# The Republic of Baseball

*June 11, 1990*

> *We are players or spectators of other sports, but citizens of baseball. Its Nielsen ratings and attendance figures go up and down, but it remains inextricably part of the American imagination.*

Ted Williams began his autobiography by saying that when he was a kid, his only ambition was to have people say, as he walked down the street, "There goes the greatest hitter who ever lived." My own autobiography could start the same way. It would end differently, though.

In this I can confidently speak for millions of American males. Every little boy has his dreams of baseball glory from the first time he feels the delicious shock in the wrists of bat smashing ball and sees the ball rocket away into the outfield, faster and farther than he knew he could propel it. That's enough to keep him going through the long summers when he's picked last in the sandlot games, assigned to bat last, and ordered to play right field, where he gets yelled at by his teammates when he lets an easy grounder roll past him.

Not to play means missing out on the common experience of the male sex. And once you get into it, it's easy to get absorbed. In Ypsilanti, Michigan, I spent long winters studying baseball statistics to while away the endless cold grey days until the snow melted. Then, around mid March, we started our new season in the park, or any empty field. At that time of year it didn't feel good to connect. In the chill, hitting the ball stung your hands, and catching it hurt worse, so that you'd suck your breath through your chattering teeth. You tried to snag the ball in the webbing of your glove, even if you were a good fielder, because having it smack your palm was almost unbearable.

Our neighborhood games were played with no more than seven boys on a team: slow pitch, no catchers, no umpires. We'd lob pitches in so that everyone could hit and put the ball in play. Anyway, we were all afraid of fast pitching, though this fear was one of those things you didn't confess, like wetting the bed or getting beaten up by your sister.

*Joe Sobran (aka "NR's slugger") poses in a Yankees uniform at Yankee Stadium to promote his cover article, "Take Me Out to the Ballgame: The Republic of Baseball," in the June 11, 1990 issue of* National Review.

But we had to face fast pitching in Little League, which turned out to be the fatal hurdle on my way to Cooperstown. To stand in there unflinching at balls whizzing in at upwards of thirty miles an hour simply required steelier nerves than mine. One who possessed such nerves was my teammate Eric Johnson, a big boy with thick glasses who could hit a speeding bullet, but couldn't catch a rolling beach ball. I can still see Eric staggering in center field, trying earnestly to get a fix on a lazy fly ball — it was a close game and the bases were loaded and oh Lord I knew what was coming. Only it was worse than I expected. The ball landed smack on the center of his skull. It was like an explosion: the ball, his cap, and his glasses blew apart simultaneously. As poor Eric groped for them all, in no special order, about seven runners streaked past me at third base.

The nonpareil of our league was Alan Bara, who at 12 had the poise and motion and narrow-eyed good looks of a big-leaguer. He already belonged on a baseball card. He'd take a perfect level cut into the ball, and it would rise on a line over the fence and just keep going. He also pitched, firing fastballs that would hit the catcher's mitt with a bang — the only pitches in the league that made that sound. Years later the local paper reported that he was hitting just over .200 in a medium-grade minor league. That gave me some inkling of what the competition in the majors must be like.

**Fan Without a Country**

My biggest treat was to go to Briggs Stadium, forty miles away, when the Yankees were in town. The best part wasn't the game. It was watching Mickey Mantle take batting practice. Other players sometimes cleared the fences. Mantle would drive ball after ball deep into the upper deck, or even over the roof. Because of him I was a Yankee fan, defying kith and kin and local loyalties.

Baseball wasn't just something we played and watched. It was something we lived. We were players, fans, historians, statisticians, philosophers, *citizens* of baseball. The game was the ground of our comradeship and the stuff of our meditations and the only future we could imagine for ourselves:

> *Lads that thought there was no more behind*
> *But such a day tomorrow as today,*
> *And to be boy eternal.*

My best friend, Terry Larson, was the same way I was, with two enviable advantages. He owned *The Official Encyclopedia of Baseball*. And his parents took the morning paper, which meant that Terry arrived at the school bus stop every morning with the latest scores and other news. One cool, sunny May morning Terry announced that Harvey Haddix had pitched 12 perfect innings the night before, only to lose in the 13th. Good old Terry always knew something I didn't. Or at least he knew it *before* I did, which gave him a certain edge, a momentary authority. We played catch, invented table games based on hitting and pitching stats, read John R. Tunis' baseball novels, and laughed at the game's great anecdotes. When our interest in baseball waned in adolescence, our friendship did too. We stayed on good terms, but we had less to talk about, no shared passion.

I quit playing and following baseball in the early Sixties, just when Roger Maris was hitting 61 home runs, Sandy Koufax was ripening into the greatest pitcher who ever lived, and the Yankees' long dominance of the game was finally coming to an end.

When I started following it again, in 1966, I felt like a Japanese soldier who had spent several seasons alone on a desert island. Returning home, as it were, I was struck by what a large part of America's daily life *talking* baseball is. A cheerful part, too. In the Detroit area it helped that the Tigers had a solid team in those days. In 1968, with Denny McLain winning 31 games, they got many of their victories in the late innings and won the World Series in wonderfully hair-raising fashion.

I needed baseball in 1968. It was gratifyingly sealed off from the real world, which was being dominated that season by Lyndon Johnson, Abbie Hoffman, and Ho Chi Minh. Baseball offered an experience that was public, but apolitical. So it has always been. A few years later, playing and just talking baseball became a chief connection with my own kids. For them, even in my twenties, I was the grizzled bard of the game, recounting the great archaic legends. Even now my twenty-year-old son Mike tells me the baseball news every morning, just like Terry used to do.

**An Accessible Past**

Baseball is inexhaustible. In loving it you are also loving many other things: summer, youth, skill, grace, camaraderie, courage, tradition, fair play, and whatever fragrances your own memory supplies.

Baseball already has its history and mythology, but its statistical lore gives it a special dimension, making its whole past accessible. And arguable.

Are today's players as good as the old ones? Much better, according to Bill Deane, a baseball historian. He figures that fewer than a third of 1901's big-leaguers could make the majors today. The talent pool is bigger now: the male population has tripled, and you don't have to be white to play. The players are notably taller. The very fact that the old heroes' stats were more extreme than today's suggests that the competition was less intense.

No pitcher today would be counseled, as the old ones were, to "save your best stuff" for crucial moments. Try to imagine a pitcher throwing forty or so complete games today, or an outfielder hauling Babe Ruth's paunch. Rogers Hornsby might still win six straight batting crowns, but nobody thinks he'd sustain a five-year average of over .400 against today's pitching (and relief pitching). It's more likely that Wade Boggs would have hit .450 in the Twenties. A new and sophisticated form of statistical analysis called "sabermetrics" is resolving many of the old debates about such matters, though some factors — like the vast improvements in fielders' gloves — elude reckoning.

One intangible though visible change is in players' attitudes. Old-timers insist that their generation was simply more dedicated to the game. A sulker like Darryl Strawberry was inconceivable in those days. Beyond that, Williams recalls that in his time players used to study and discuss the techniques of hitting endlessly during off-days; now they don't. DiMaggio has said similar things, more bemused than querulous. The frequency of the strikeout in modern baseball shows the declining premium placed on just making contact with the ball. Williams and DiMaggio both hit home runs nearly as often as they struck out. Last year's home-run leaders, Fred McGriff and Kevin Mitchell, hit 36 and 47 homers but fanned 132 and 115 times.

Has big money taken the edge off the desire to excel? Maybe. Probably. But how much? Unanswerable. The highest salary now is around $4 million. Even adjusting for inflation, that tops the $5,000 Ralph Kiner got in 1946, when he led the National League in homers with 23. He also got $4,000 in 1947, when he hit 51, after the

Pirates' general manager had refused his request for a raise with airtight logic: "We finished last with you, we can finish last without you." Mantle generated millions in profits for the Yankees when he won the Triple Crown in 1956, for which he was paid $32,500. When he went in to negotiate a raise, the general manager, George Weiss, pulled out a private detective's detailed report on Mantle's nightlife, remarking what a pity it would be if it fell into Mrs. Mantle's hands. (And they complain about George Steinbrenner.)

It's hard to begrudge the players their new prosperity. But there's no question they are allowed to be more temperamental than formerly, thanks to free agency. This has gotten to be a joke. In 1976 the Tigers put 47-year-old Al Cicotte on their roster for four days, strictly as a favor (he needed four games to be eligible for a pension). He hadn't pitched since 1962, and his circumference required a specially tailored uniform. When his pal Ralph Houk, the Tigers' manager, jocosely assured local sportswriters that Cicotte probably wouldn't be seeing much action, Cicotte roared: "Play me or trade me!"

When comparing the quality of today's baseball with that of yesteryear's, it's important to bear in mind the St. Louis Browns. Through most of their existence, the Browns occupied a rung somewhere between seventh place and the Gulag Archipelago. But it's an ill wind that blows no man good, and World War II, by draining baseball of most of its talent for three years, reshuffled the standings so thoroughly that in 1944 the Browns won their first and only pennant. (When a newly captured American pilot related this news to his fellow Americans in a German POW camp, they assumed he must be a German plant. He was ostracized and tormented until a subsequent captive confirmed his story.)

At least nobody argues that baseball was at its best during the war. The majors were filled with athletes who had been classified 4-F by their draft boards, and the Browns had the distinction of using a one-armed outfielder named Pete Gray. After the war, they once used a midget as a pinch-hitter — an inspiration of owner Bill Veeck, who himself had only one leg. Veeck tried to rebuild the team by replacing veterans with young players, but that effort came a cropper when, before one game with the Yankees, the Browns' hard-bitten manager, Zack Taylor, found that several of his rookies were missing. He finally spotted them over in the Yankee dugout, seeking autographs. "Damnedest thing I ever saw," Taylor snorted.

After finishing last again in 1953, the Browns were sold and moved to Baltimore, leaving behind the most dismal peacetime record in baseball history. If they had existed during the Hundred Years War, they might have been formidable.

Anyway, when someone tries to tell you baseball was better in the old days, ask him if he's including the St. Louis Browns. The Browns' pitching staff alone helps explain why there used to be .400 hitters back then. If they put an asterisk beside Maris' 61 home runs for having been hit over 162 games, they should put one beside DiMaggio's 56-game hitting streak for having been compiled against the likes of Eldon Auker, who that year gave up 268 hits (and 85 walks) in a mere 216 innings, with a 5.50 ERA to boot.

**Good Books, Lousy Movies**

Baseball has inspired many good books and lousy movies. The latter include several recent hits: *The Natural, Bull Durham,* and *Field of Dreams.* They all have essentially the same fault: they don't respect baseball. They rely on the smirky, the maudlin, the miraculous to generate emotion. They try to *force* the audience to react, going for the guffaw or the lump in the throat without earning honest sentiment. In *Bull Durham,* the team slut displays her sophisticated awareness of quantum physics by repeatedly using the phrase "quantum physics." She makes no mention of Heidegger or Derrida, from which you can safely infer that the scriptwriter has never heard of them, because he'd surely have stuck their names in too. It's that sort of movie.

Not that a baseball movie has to display expert knowledge of the game in order to be good. *Eight Men Out*, a straightforward account of how the 1919 World Series was fixed, is an honorable failure (it's just a little flat and unfocused). But a baseball drama has to find its power in the normal achievements and emotions of baseball itself, without impossible heroics or smutty farce. Winning a close game is dramatic enough to hold a crowd's attention in a stadium, and ought to be able to do the same in a theater. Tunis' boys' books found plenty of tension in the typical situations of sport: conquering fear, coming back from an injury, putting the team ahead of yourself.

The baseball book of the season is George Will's *Men at Work*, a study of what Will calls baseball's "complexities and nuances," formerly known as the fine points of the game. (If they kept stats on fancy words, "nuances" would be crowding "parameters" for first place in 1990.) Whatever you want to call them, Will writes about them with a fine eye for the telling statistic and a deep sense of what statistics don't tell you. Like all the best baseball writing, the book assumes that baseball deserves intelligent attention and doesn't need to be talked down to.

In his introductory and concluding pages, Will flags a little. He argues, for instance, that being an intelligent fan is "a form of appreciating that is good for the individual's soul, and hence for society." Feeble rationalization. Like any true baseball lover, Will wouldn't care if baseball dissolved your moral fiber and got you arrested by the secret police. Baseball justifies itself, like music. It doesn't have to be *good* for you, like a sermon, into the bargain.

Nevertheless, baseball does have its own kind of moral appeal. It's free of the frequent ugliness of other team sports: the fights and fouls and pilings-on that are characteristic of football, basketball, and hockey, if not intrinsic to them. Bad-conduct penalties of any kind are exceptional in baseball. You (almost) never see a play in baseball canceled by a penalty — and even the (almost) is necessitated only by the notorious "pine-tar incident." (Every fan remembers it.)

Baseball is a deeply orderly game. The distinctiveness of its component actions — pitching, hitting, fielding, and base-running — makes them available to separate attention, measurement, analysis, and judgment. Every player's contribution to every play is recorded and given value. The statistics are rarely misleading. If you want to know who the American League's best second baseman of the Thirties was, well, as Casey Stengel used to say, "You could look it up." Try that with defensive linemen.

Other sports thrill; baseball also absorbs. It's the most discussable game, and it's the national pastime largely because we can talk about it so volubly long after we can play it. No other sport binds the generations the way baseball does.

Because it's so thoroughly recorded, baseball has a genuine history. It also has a continuity that the other major team sports don't have. "The NFL keeps changing the most basic rules," Thomas

Boswell observes. "Most blocking now would have been illegal use of the hands in Jim Parker's time. How do we compare eras when the sport never stays the same?" In fact, none of the other three sports is the same game it was as recently as the Fifties, for all sorts of reasons. Wilt Chamberlain's season scoring records will never be broken, simply because nobody will ever again play against as many white players as Chamberlain did. (If you want a sure-fire laugh, ask a basketball fan whether Michael Jordan is as great as George Mikan.)

The statistical discreteness of individual performance, set against the game's stable history, gives achievement in baseball a permanence and stature other sports can seldom confer. And even racial integration hasn't devalued the old records; in fact, most fans — including experts — doubt that Henry Aaron was a greater slugger than the man whose supreme record he broke. Lawrence Ritter reckons that with as many times at bat as Aaron, Ruth would have hit 1,064 home runs. Be that as it may, heroism in baseball is more perduring than in other American sports, and does much to account for the splendid literature baseball has produced. Nearly every fan has read John Updike's description of Williams' last game.

**Old and Ever New**

And of course baseball is always with us, 162 games a year. We get to know the players, unhidden by helmets and shoulder pads. Nobody calls it an "upset" when the worst team beats the best. Old as it is, baseball is forever making news. It just keeps rolling along, and even the Pete Rose scandal can't pollute it.

Racial integration has worked better in baseball than in any other area of American life. The game has an unforced racial and ethnic balance. It succeeds because the rules are really impartial. Baseball is a refuge from "social justice." What it offers instead is simple fairness. There are no "racist" balls and strikes, no "affirmative action" balls and strikes, only balls and strikes.

The umpires don't care who deserves to win on moral, progressive, or demographic grounds. Their role is modest but crucial, and would be corrupted if they brought any supposed Higher Purpose to their work. They care only about the rules. The Supreme Court could learn from them.

The rules themselves are remarkably few. They're designed only to facilitate performance, never to hinder it, beyond maintaining a certain equilibrium between offense and defense. In baseball we enjoy what we no longer find in politics: the Western genius for rule-making.

A large part of that genius lies in changing the rules as seldom as possible. Baseball is older than the income tax, but its rules can still be printed in a small pamphlet; the tax code runs to several thousand pages. If you've played baseball you can intuit most of the rules without reading them, and you don't need a lawyer to explain them to you. They arise from the game's internal logic and never seem to have been superimposed for alien or interested purposes.

In politics, men are elected to bend the rules in someone's favor. It shouldn't surprise us when they break them too. A key difference between baseball and democracy is that in baseball the winners don't get to rewrite the rules. And it never occurs to the losers to blame the rules for their losses. Our deepest norms of order can still be seen in operation on the diamond when they've been adulterated everywhere else. Baseball is our Utopia — not in assuring us of the victories we dream of, but in guaranteeing ideal conditions even of defeat.

# Choosing Death

review of
*What Ever Happened to the Human Race?*
(Revell, 256 pp.) by Everett Koop and Francis Schaeffer

*February 8, 1980*

The sickness of the West is very deep. This book makes that appallingly clear. The authors — a theologian and a pediatrician — discuss three evil practices that strike at the core values of our civilization: abortion, infanticide, and euthanasia. As you read you are sickened by their convincing argument that all three are symptoms of the cheapening of life by the anti-human ideology that calls itself "humanism."

I vividly remember the Finkbine case in the early Sixties, when Sherry Finkbine, pregnant with a Thalidomide baby, elected to go to Sweden for an abortion. It caused a national uproar. A priest wrote to *Time* suggesting, "Why not wait until the baby is born, and then, if it is defective, kill it? That would be more consequential."

Today it is routine to abort healthy babies. The good priest's *reductio* has lost its force. As for defective infants, many experts now openly advocate letting them die of starvation, if need be. The question has even arisen whether healthy babies should always be granted a right to live once they are born. Two Nobel Prize-winners, James Watson and Francis Crick, have independently suggested that no such right be assumed until a baby has reached an arbitrarily determined age: three days, say.

The authors (and Dr. Koop speaks from wide acquaintance with his profession) contend that infanticide is already widely practiced. So was abortion, long before it was respectable to argue publicly for it. And of course it takes less technical refinement to kill a child outside than inside the womb.

We have supped full with horrors, and I suppose nobody will faint at the news. A pity. But it is worth bearing in mind that evil practices outrun the reasons adduced for them. A few years ago we heard all the hard-case rationales for abortion: cases like Mrs. Finkbine's made it a necessary evil. The next thing we knew, the hard cases had multiplied to include economic difficulties. Then abortion was a matter of personal choice, neither good nor evil in itself. Finally — at least it seemed like the last stop — abortion became a positive right, in certain cases a desirable thing.

We're beyond that now. With the case for infanticide, the "reformers" have left behind the notion that only a woman's sovereignty over her own body is at stake. People want to get rid of their children: that's the long and the short of it. When moral inhibitions are removed, the helpless lose. And some doctors are equating technical expertise with the requisite moral authority to guide, or to make unilaterally, the decision whether to kill a given infant.

Religion is in decline. Humanism in various forms holds sway. Mass media can supplant tradition with fashion overnight. A new practice can become thinkable and then acceptable, even routine, with astonishing rapidity. Dr. Koop has been trying for years to alert us (I was incredulous at first) that pediatrics has been increasingly given over to a gentlemen's agreement that certain defective infants should be done away with.

But as the abortion issue shows, the definition of "defective" has quickly broadened to mean anything not wanted by people in a position to kill. There is the case of a young couple who asked for a prenatal test to determine the sex of the child they were expecting: they said they feared a boy would be hemophiliac. When the test showed it was a girl, they admitted they actually wanted a boy, because they *preferred* a boy. The girl was aborted.

Most of the ostensible moral concerns, then, are rationalizations. Yet once a previously taboo practice is accepted, it can acquire new dimensions. The acceptance of eugenic tampering has led at least one doctor (a woman) to call for mandatory sterilization of all people who have had two children. If they manage to have a third, that third child should be sterilized.

The idealistic blueprints don't work out. Legal abortion was supposed to eliminate illegal abortion. But illegal abortion has increased. Legal abortion was supposed to lessen the child abuse resulting from unwanted children; but the reported incidence of child abuse has soared. Schaeffer and Koop theorize that the lessened value of a child's life has invited many parents to think, perversely, that since they were kind enough not to kill the child before birth, they can't be blamed too much for severity to it afterward. (You're lucky to be alive at all, you brat.)

Euthanasia for old folks follows a similar course. Once it is allowed as the subject's option, pressure will mount for its exercise, until the subject himself may no longer be the one to make the choice. The act of institutionalizing euthanasia may seem, at first, to be what it claims to be: a simple expansion of personal freedom. But selfish people won't be slow to make the deeper inference implicit in it — that life isn't very valuable. Abortion and infanticide will already have provided precedents for some people deciding on behalf of others. If people shouldn't be burdened with unwanted children, why with unwanted parents? And once the family structure has been gutted, why not let state experts handle things rationally?

The authors point back to genocide as an application of the notion that some people have the right to pronounce on the humanity of others. In my judgment they might point ahead to it as well. Of course it's unfashionable now. But given the moral fluidity of the modern situation, I see no reason why it shouldn't make a comeback. The actual exercise of new prerogatives seldom remains with the people it was intended for; the vulgarians almost always wind up taking it over. Socialism, as Hayek long ago argued, tends to terminate in rule by thugs, who have a way of displacing the refined experts.

*What Ever Happened to the Human Race?* is, literally, evangelical. Its second half offers Protestant Christianity as the solution to the moral breakdown. As far as it goes, it's a good prima facie argument. It suggests, along the lines followed earlier by C.S. Lewis (and many others), that scientism itself is an artificial mode of consciousness, and that a full response to man's existence inevitably turns to God, not man, as the measure of all things, and specifically to Christ as the revelation of God. At this point the book directly appeals to personal response; a reviewer's judgment is of little value. But the first half, at any rate, will leave few readers unshaken: the authors see too clearly what is really happening, as opposed to what the "reformers" say is happening. One wonders how a West so decadent can plausibly stand up to any external foe.

# Afterword

Joe and I were walking to a party in Foggy Bottom once, when a scruffy white guy offered to sell us a case of beer he happened to have on his person. The proposed salesman was the sort of fellow who could have been either a scofflaw or just a guy who somehow ended up with an extra case of beer. I would have kept walking, but Joe politely stopped as if he wasn't aware that it is not considered ill-mannered to keep moving when a stranger approaches you on the street and offers to sell you something. Joe was unfailingly polite.

Joe made some inquiries vaguely directed at determining if the beer had been stolen, but, for whatever reason, decided against the purchase. He was perfectly nice about it. As we were walking away, still unsure of the beer's provenance, the vagrant/honest entrepreneur started cursing Joe, who cheerfully noted: "Well, now we know it was stolen."

Joe loved it when people gave themselves away like this, though it was more often liberals than vagrants he caught doing it.

In his column on the 1982 nuclear freeze rally in New York, Joe set forth the desperate attempt of the media — what he called "the hive" — to portray the event as completely bipartisan, a "broad coalition," encompassing people of all political stripes.

He proceeded to list the speakers interrupting the music at the rally: "Robert Drinan, Bella Abzug, Helen Caldicott, Coretta Scott King, William Sloane Coffin, Elizabeth Holtzman, Barry Commoner. Speakers, need one point out, representing all ideologies."

Joe's specialty was to make blindingly simple points that would cut through mountains of sophistry. Once you heard them no amount of fancy footwork could make that particular liberal humbug work again.

In response to the cant about the marchers simply opposing nuclear war (which then-president Reagan apparently supported, as evidenced by his military build-up) Joe exposed the fraud with a question:

"A libertarian might have suggested dismantling not only the Pentagon but also the whole range of social programs. Would the speakers have accepted this deal, if it would avert nuclear war?

Sacrifice even socialism for peace? To ask the question is to realize at once their real agenda."

(It should be noted that documents released since the fall of the Soviet Union have now established that the nuclear freeze movement was instigated and directed from behind the Iron Curtain, mostly by East Germany.)

Joe could say in a sentence what most writers would need an entire column to express: "Little of the anti-Reagan rhetoric came through, except an occasional exasperated suggestion that the problem was that Reagan doesn't seem to appreciate what nuclear war would *mean*."

He quoted liberals not simply to laugh at them, but to show what was being hidden.

Of the hive's obsessive desire to describe the "Peace" supporters as a "broad coalition," for example, Joe wrote: "The *Times* knows that the progressive cause advances fastest, in the long run, when it proceeds under the cover of conservative forms. The coded euphemism is all-important."

He was like the guy warning about a pickpocket while the rest of us were transfixed by the commotion being created by the pickpocket's accomplice.

While others laughed at various PC locutions and rules, Joe saw the long-term goal:

"We're being nudged into a series of little repudiations of the Western patrimony. The changing rules embody this. Profanity and obscenity are okay; but new taboos forbid 'racism,' 'sexism,' and other Politically Incorrect attitudes. (Religion is purely optional, but bigotry must be 'eliminated.')"

The liberal re-ordering of the world was always there, but mostly unnoticed until Joe named and defined this or that aspect of the liberal *Weltanschauung*: the "hive"; liberal "etiquette" ("A sectarian ideology has triumphed when it has turned itself into an etiquette that all must observe"); and the media's "super-story" (liberal myths sustained by cherry-picking the news for front-page stories).

Perhaps because he saw liberals so clearly, he was never angry, more anthropological. He understood liberals so much better than they understood themselves.

Reviewing a feminist book, Joe describes it as "less a book than a symptom," saying that if "you read between the lines — which in this case sure beats reading the lines — you quickly see that the point of the book is to congratulate 'educated' Catholics on their achievement of Correct Attitudes." These Correct Attitudes, he said, "were always quick-frozen bits of liberal dogma. You didn't have to do any thinking; you simply put the relevant attitude on like a hat, and presto! you were fashionable."

His complaint with the ACLU differed from that of other conservatives — and not because he had a corpuscle that would get a thrill from saying "both sides" were wrong, as is the case with so many conservatives.

While admitting that the ACLU "takes a liberal political line whose predictability is only occasionally broken by its willingness to move a little ahead of the herd, as on kiddie porn," his principal complaint was both more true and more insulting:

"The ACLU is an outfit for mediocrities who like to think of themselves as mavericks. A real maverick won't join an organization with an orthodoxy about political issues over which disagreement is natural and consensus rare. He won't kid himself that all his political preferences (and those of his friends) dovetail nicely with the Constitution. He knows that life is more problematic than that. He realizes that there are tensions between desire and convenience, between what he says he always wants and what he actually wants on Tuesday. The real maverick doesn't try to paper over these ironies; he savors them, even in himself."

For most normal people, cool reason is not the immediate response to liberal attacks on basic moral precepts that we never thought we'd have to defend, e.g., not killing humans in the womb, why gay men should not be taking 14 year-old boy scouts on camping trips, the purpose of marriage, and common decency.

It was Joe's sang-froid in the face of such lunacy that allowed him to be so clear-eyed in his refutations.

Writing about *Playboy* magazine's indignant denunciation of a Supreme Court obscenity ruling, Joe highlighted the nugget of the argument: "The obscene is a subjective concept, existing only in the minds of the beholders." To this Joe asked: If "obscenity" is purely subjective, then what about the words *Playboy* chose to attack the decision? The editorial also said, for example, that "there are ultimately 200,000,000 qualified judges of obscenity in the U.S. and ... each has a right to his opinion." This, Joe said, raised the question: "[W]hat can 'qualified' possibly mean? or 'obscenity'? or 'right'?"

Because of my work as well as my personal sentiments on the matter, Joe and I talked a lot about the verbal sleights of hand of the pornography-defenders. One time, he made an argument that was right in front of me, but I had never noticed until he said it. Liberals always triumphantly assert that "pornography" is completely beyond definition, but at the same time swear up and down to oppose child pornography. So how do they know what "child pornography" is, if "pornography" is impossible to identify? The only difference is the age of the participants, something that is perfectly objective. To explain to a liberal what "pornography" is, just tell them it's child pornography with adults.

Joe was the master of catching these champion desecrators of life in their own contradictions. Here, he asks why rape is still so horrifying to the sexual liberationists if casual sex is not:

"The lasting torment of rape victims, about which we hear so much, ought to prove this. Physically, rape is no worse than a severe beating. But the horror of it lies in a deeper violation than mere pain can inflict. There is something jarring in the contrast between the 'trauma' of rape as we hear it described (accurately enough, no doubt) and the general trivialization of Eros. Why in one case alone are we supposed to assume, and accept as normal, that deep nerves are struck? If casual Sex is not to be experienced as defiling, why should a rape seem so lastingly degrading? Do rape victims just happen to be women with more than their share of hangups? Or is it that the experience of rape gives the lie to the ideology of Sex?"

But you know all these quotes from reading this book, whence they came. I have quoted Joe extensively because to describe being with him requires focusing on the elegance of his mind. It didn't matter if he was talking about a Batman movie, abortion or Shakespeare. He was constantly thinking — especially of intellectual traps and jokes.

Still, inasmuch as this is an Afterword, the reader probably wants to know more about Joe, the man. He was as loyal a friend as could be imagined, old-school chivalrous, warm and funny, generous to a fault — including with his ideas — and genuinely happy about his friends' successes, even in writing, a freakishly rare sentiment among writers. (And no, he was not constantly muttering about Jews. Although in his last few years, he was constantly muttering about that imposter, William Shakespeare.)

What was most fun about Joe was his delight in ideas. Probably because so much "conventional wisdom" was obviously bunk, no ideas frightened him. In fact, the more unconventional they were, the more interested he was. Novel theories were just a new Rubik's cube for him to solve.

I learned so much about writing from Joe, both by direct instruction — he told me to write as if I were writing to a friend — and observation: he'd try out his arguments in conversation, so that before he ever sat at his typewriter, the entire column, beginning to end, would be in his head (and mine). Just by being around him, you'd start to reason differently, to question accepted dogmas.

Which is why I, and all of Joe's friends, were so depressed when he died a couple years ago. We lost not only a genuine, completely selfless friend, but also an endless source of intellectual inspiration.

*Ann Coulter*
*May 3, 2012*

"My enemies are always welcome to quote anything I say, if they dare." –Joe Sobran

# Joseph Sobran

Joseph Sobran (1946-2010) was an important paleoconservative Christian writer and sought-after speaker of the late twentieth and early twenty-first centuries. Often compared to G.K. Chesterton and H.L. Mencken, Sobran was praised for giving insightful spins on politics, the culture war, the overreaching state, Lincoln, and Shakespeare. Sobran predicted years in advance the war against Christian society, the culture of death, the decline of society, the abandonment of the Constitution, and the perils of government intervention in our lives.

If you had asked Joseph Sobran to describe himself, he would have said simply that he was a writer. That was his extraordinary, God-given talent, his mission, and the purpose of his life.

Born in Detroit in 1946, he grew up in Ypsilanti, Michigan. He received a B.A. in English from Eastern Michigan University and did graduate studies in English, specializing in Shakespeare. From 1969 to 1970 he taught English on a fellowship, and lectured on Shakespeare.

From 1971 to 1993, he worked as a writer and editor for *National Review* magazine. This volume has a sampling of those articles. From 1979 to 1991, "Joe," as his friends called him, was a commentator on CBS Radio's "Spectrum" series.

For nearly 30 years, he wrote a bi-weekly column, which was syndicated initially by the Los Angeles Times Syndicate and later by Universal Press Syndicate and Griffin Internet Syndicate.

For some 20 years, he wrote the weekly column "Washington Watch" for *The Wanderer*, a weekly Catholic newspaper. In addition, he penned numerous essays and articles for many other publications over a writing career spanning nearly 40 years, including *Human Life Review, Celebrate Life!* and *Chronicles* magazine. During his career, he was a popular speaker and lecturer throughout the country, and appeared on many TV and radio talk shows.

For 13 years, from 1994 to 2007, he was editor of *SOBRAN'S: The Real News of the Month,* a monthly newsletter of his essays and columns published by Griffin Communications.

Joe Sobran's book, *Alias Shakespeare: Solving the Greatest Literary Mystery of All Time* (The Free Press, 1997), argued the case for Edward de Vere as the true author of the Shakespeare plays and sonnets. He also wrote five books in the series *Shakespeare Explained* (Marshall Cavendish, 2008-2010).

There have been several anthologies of his work, including *Single Issues: Essays on the Crucial Social Questions* (The Human Life Press, New York, 1983); *Hustler: The Clinton Legacy* (Griffin Communications, 2000; and FGF Books, 2016); and *Subtracting Christianity: Essays on American Culture and Society* (FGF Books, 2015).

Joe Sobran died on September 30, 2010. He is buried at St. Andrew's Cemetery in Vienna, Virginia. Some of the many tributes that appeared about him after his death can be read at fgfBooks.com.

*The publication of this book was made possible, in large part, by the following generous benefactors:*

Hans J. Burgdorf
Jeffrey P. Buol
John and Ann Cianflone
Christopher Condon
Dale Jr. and Mary Crowley
Richard and Constance Culley
Robert L. Hale
Michael Hartnett
Michael Hattwick, MD
Parke Harvey
Daniel P. Hayes
Robert D. Hurt, DDS
Erwin Jaumann
Rachel Kennedy
Rod Miller
Michael A. Peroutka
Stephen G. Peroutka
Kian Keith Putbrese
The John and Lillian Seigfreid Family
Alex Sepkus
Peggy and Bennett Smith
R.J. Stove
Taki Theodoracopulous
Jon Basil Utley
Lewis V. Walker
Howard and Eleanor Walsh
Mr. and Mrs. Sean P. Walsh

# Index

2 Live Crew  6
*1984*  98, 139

**A**

Aaron, Henry  154
abolition of man  11
Abzug, Bella  3, 42, 159
academia  9, 101, 109
Adam  88
Aeschylus  34, 118
affirmative action  13, 28, 109, 154
Afghanistan  36, 42, 95
Africa  13, 25, 28, 69
Afro-American  22
Agnew, Spiro  16
*Alias Shakespeare*  iv, xv, 165
Allen, Percy  117
*All in the Family*  102, 108
Alvarez, Patricia  xviii
America, American  vi, xi, xii, xvi, 3, 4, 7, 13, 14, 17, 21, 22, 23, 25, 27, 29, 30, 31, 35, 37, 39, 42, 46, 47, 48, 55, 56, 58, 60, 70, 73, 75, 79, 84, 87, 88, 94, 96, 100, 102, 107, 109, 138, 142, 146, 149, 151, 153, 154
American Civil Liberties Union (ACLU)  47, 48, 161
Americanization  84
American League  153
Americans for Democratic Action (ADA)  39
Amos 'n' Andy  108
anachronism  109
anarchist, anarchy  43
Anderson, John  93
Andropov, Yuri  94, 95
Antony and Cleopatra  8
anti-Catholicism  59, 143
antisemitism  104
apolitical  39, 45, 90, 149
Aquinas, Thomas  11, 36, 59, 79
Archie Bunker  108

Aristotle  34, 107, 129
art  24, 25, 42, 54, 56, 68, 99, 100, 103, 104, 105, 107, 128, 130
arts  100, 102, 103, 104, 105, 109, 138
Aslan  127
atheist  74
Atwater, Lee  116
Augustine, Augustinian  86, 88–90
Auker, Eldon  152

# B

baby, babies  43, 47, 59, 125, 156
Babylon  88
Bach  78
Bacon, Francis  117
Baez, Joan  15
Baptists  42, 76, 77
Bara, Alan  148
barbarians, barbarism  30, 54, 104, 110
baseball  22, 146, 148–155
Bauer, Peter  83
Baxter, Ted  58
Beard, Charles  79
Beatles  15
Beatty, Jack  22
Beaumont, Francis  118
beehive  13, 94
Benthamite  81
Benton, Barbi  67
Berkeley, Bishop  27
Berlin Wall  30, 31
Berlin, Irving  114, 116
Bethell, Tom  v, vi, xvi, xviii, 94
bias  xi, 5, 23, 52, 53, 54, 96, 102
Bible  23, 38
bigot, bigoted  20, 29, 108
bigotry  4, 21, 29, 102, 106, 108, 109, 160
bigotry, religious  102
Bill of Rights  47
birth control  9, 10, 11, 74
Blackmun, Harry  138
blacks, Negroes  20, 21, 43, 44, 69, 70, 87, 102, 105, 107, 108

Blood, Sweat and Tears  15
Boggs, Wade  150
Bok, Edward  84
Borgnine, Ernest  125
bosom  100, 122, 140
Boswell, Thomas  154
Bowles, Chester  3, 13, 14
Boyd, Fr. Ian  132, 134
Boyle, James  138, 139
Brando, Marlon  64, 111, 112
Brennan, William  138
Breslin, Jimmy  21, 143
Brezhnev  94, 95, 96
British National Theatre  104
Broadway  104
*Brown* vs. *Board of Education*  28
Brown, Claude  84
Browne, Jackson  42
Bruce, Lenny  65
Brutus  82
Buchanan, Patrick J.  v, vi, xiii, xix
Buckley, William F., Buckley, Bill  xv, 21, 22, 27, 79, 85, 97, 101
Buckley, Priscilla  85
Buddhist  13
*Bull Durham*  152
Burgess, Anthony  126
Burke, Edmund  50, 71
Burnham, James  ix, xii, 2, 36, 77, 79, 85, 86, 97, 98, 144
busing  47
Butterfield, Herbert  4

# C

Caesar  82, 103, 111
Calabrese, O.P., Br. Mario  xviii
Caldicott, Helen  42, 159
Caliban  105
Canovan, Margaret  133
cant  3, 29, 50, 159
Capitalism  5, 41, 81–83, 87
*Capitalism, Sources of Hostility*  81
capital punishment  81

Carson, Johnny  100
Carter, Jimmy  xii, 55, 91, 92, 93
Casanova  9
Cassio  130, 136
Catholic(s)  9, 25, 36, 37, 42, 59, 62, 65, 72, 73, 74, 75, 76, 77, 84, 90,
    126, 132, 141, 142, 143, 144
Catholic Church, Church  4, 9, 25, 33, 35, 59, 65, 73, 74, 75, 76, 84, 87,
    138, 141, 142, 143, 144
*Catholicism and Modernity: Confrontation or Capitulation?*  141
*Catholics and American Politics*  75
Caulfield, Holden  111
CBS  xvii, 56, 94, 127, 165
censor, censored, censorship  14, 95, 100–104, 109
centralization of power  50
centralized state power  13
Chamberlain, John  86
Chamberlain, Wilt  154
Chaplin, Charlie  131
chastity  35, 142
Chesterton, G.K.  xvi, 132–134
Chicago  xvii, 64, 68, 78, 79
child, children  9, 10–13, 24, 39, 44, 45, 60, 63, 72, 73, 74, 77, 82, 89,
    103, 106, 108, 126, 127, 156, 157, 158, 162
child abuse  13, 157
Chile  13, 25
China, Chinese  10, 30, 42, 83, 88, 89, 144
Christ  36, 37, 65, 73, 90, 126, 127, 142, 143, 158
Christendom College  xvi
Christian(s)  12, 25, 33, 34, 35, 37, 38, 89, 90, 104, 105
*Christian Humanism*  33, 34
Christianity  34, 89, 158
CIA  76
Cicotte, Al  151
*City of God, The*  89
civil libertarian  13
civil liberties  14, 36, 48, 75, 76
civil rights  6, 13, 20, 21, 25, 29
civil society  11
Clark, Ramsey  81
Clayburgh, Jill  43
coalition  43, 45, 46, 159, 160

Cocker, Joe 15
Coffin, William Sloane 43, 159
Cold War xii, 90
cold-war rhetoric 42, 46
collectivism, collectivist 4, 82, 83
color-blind society 28
*Coming Defeat of Communism, The* 99
*Commentary* 1, 2, 75
Commoner, Barry 43, 159
communication, communications 54, 55, 83, 102, 107
Communism, Communist 3, 25, 26, 30, 31, 37, 38, 39, 41, 42, 44, 48, 53, 71, 76, 86, 88, 89, 90, 92, 94, 98, 99, 102, 144
Communist countries 53, 144
Communist Party 39, 41, 42, 48
*Confessions of a Conservative* 84, 85, 89
*Confessions of a White Racist* 84
conservatism, conservative xi, 1, 2, 3, 4, 5, 45, 78, 80, 85, 86, 87, 90, 92, 101, 102, 108, 109, 113, 123, 160
*Conservative Mind, The* 79
Constitution 47, 48, 51, 161
Constitutionalist 5
consumer 95
consumerist 13
contraception 9, 10, 74, 133
contraceptive devices 9
Cooke, Janet 23, 24
Coriolanus 109, 136
Correct Attitudes 76, 77, 161
*Cosby Show* 22
Coulter, Ann iv, v, vi, xix, 163
countercultural, counterculture xi, 15, 17, 18, 64
covet, covetousness 81
Cox, Harvey 65, 144
Creedence Clearwater Revival 15
Crick, Francis 156
crime 8, 21, 22, 47, 63, 81
criminal 109
Cronkite, Walter 52, 54, 56
Crosby, Bing 15, 112
Crosby, Stills, Nash and Young 15
C.S. Lewis 11, 79, 80, 82, 108, 127, 132, 158
Cuddihy, John Murray 29

cultural, culture  4, 18, 44, 50, 53, 54, 64, 65, 67, 68, 71, 73, 78, 84, 85, 103, 106, 108, 109, 111, 112, 113, 138, 145
Cuomo, Governor Mario  21
Curry, Jack  18

# D

Dante  108
Dark Ages  33
Dean, James  111
Deane, Bill  150
death penalty  81
Debs, Eugene  10
decorum  50, 100, 104, 108
defamation  27
Desdemona  8, 130
de Vere, Edward  117, 119, 138, 139
Dickens  108, 124, 133
DiMaggio  150, 152
Dionysian, Dionysus  xi, 15, 16, 18
disarmament  25, 41, 43
discrimination  4, 20, 22, 101
discrimination, liberal  101
*Distributivism*  132
diversity  44, 48, 94
Divine Right of Kings  11
divorce  8, 11, 12, 138
Dogberry  123
Donahue, Phil  58, 59, 60
Donahue, William  47
Donne  7
Dos Passos, John  79
Drinan, Robert  33, 42, 159
drug abuse  18
*Dude*  61, 67
Dukakis, Michael  47
Dylan, Bob  15, 112, 113

# E

Earl of Montgomery  119-120
Earl of Oxford  x, xii, 117, 119, 120, 138-140
Earl of Pembroke  119
Earl of Southampton  119

Eastman, Max  10
economic, economics, economy  xi, 6, 10, 15, 21, 43, 53, 54, 76, 78, 81, 82, 83, 93, 95, 106, 157
Edgar  132
*Ed Sullivan Show*  115
education  12, 49, 59, 76, 77, 129
Educational Testing Service  102
egalitarian(s)  13
*Eight Men Out*  152
elections  87, 88, 89
elites, elitism  xii, 85, 87, 143, 165
English  xii, 29, 50, 54, 101, 117, 121, 128, 129, 130, 132, 135, 140, 165
Enlightenment  33, 82
environmentalism, environmentalist  13
envy  81, 82
Eros  9, 162
*Esquire*  62, 87
ethnocentrism  69, 110
eugenics  133
euphemism(s), euphemistic  30, 39, 45, 66, 160
euthanasia  156, 158
Ezrahi, Yaron  23

## F

Fallows, James  92
family  10, 11, 12, 13, 14, 69, 82, 88, 95, 108, 121, 133, 158, 167
fascist(s)  5, 36, 37, 102, 109
FBI  76, 79
Feder, Don  21
feminism, feminist  10, 13, 72, 160
Feuer, Lewis  82
First Amendment  28, 29, 47, 49, 56, 95
forced labor  89
Forsberg, Randall  40, 45
Francis, Sam  xviii
Franciscan Herald Press  33
freedom, personal freedom  11, 14, 32, 47, 51, 70, 99, 103, 143, 158
freedom of speech, free speech  29, 51
freedom of the press  47, 51
free love  xi, 8, 12, 18
free market  56, 86

free press 51, 54, 95
free speech 6, 29
*Freeman, The* 86
Friedman, Milton 2
Friedman, Thomas 22

## G

gay rights 47
genocide 8, 16, 158
German, Germany 10, 31, 32, 66, 78, 79, 151, 160
ghetto 24, 84, 77, 85
Gielgud, John 111
Glazer, Nathan 83
Gnosticism 33
God xvii, 11, 34, 59, 60, 63, 73, 74, 88, 89, 122, 125, 127, 158
*God and Man at Yale* 79
Golding, Arthur 119
Goldman, Emma 10
Gollanez, Victor 79
*Gone With the Wind* 69
Gospel 65, 125, 126, 127, 142
Grateful Dead, The 15
Gray, Pete 151
Great Society 26
Great Wall of China 30
Greeley, Andrew 77
Greene, Robert 121
Griffin, Fran v, vi, xix
Gromyko 98
Guardini, Romano 79
gun control 47
Guthrie, Arlo 15

## H

Haddix, Harvey 149
Hadrian's Wall 30
Haley, Alex 69
*Hamlet,* Hamlet 8, 109, 111, 119, 120, 129, 135, 136, 140
Hanna, Mary T. 75–77
Harvard 75, 78, 81
Harvard University Press 75

hate  3, 5, 23, 45, 81, 82, 83, 123, 124, 126
*Hawaii Five-O*  109
Haydn  104
Hayek, Friedrich von  51, 56, 158
Hazlitt, Henry  86
hedonism  74, 144
Hefner, Hugh  ix, 61–68
Hendrix, Jimi  xi, 15, 16
*Henry V*  135
Hentoff, Nat  113
Hindu  13
hippie  xi, 15, 16, 17, 19
historical guilt  88
Hitchcock, Alfred  31
Hitchcock, James  33, 37, 89, 141, 142, 143, 144
Hitler  66, 78, 132
Hive, The  14, 39, 40, 42, 44, 45, 46, 94, 159, 160
Ho Chi Minh  149
Hoffman, Abbie  xi, 16, 18, 42, 149
Holmes, Oliver Wendell  40, 109, 132, 133
Holtzman, Elizabeth  43, 159
Homer  34
homophobic  27
homosexual, homosexuality  13, 58, 136
Hooker  11
Hoover, J. Edgar  16
Horatio  8
Horne, Jed  30, 32
Hornsby, Rogers  150
hostage(s)  55, 91, 92
hostage crisis  91
Houk, Ralph  151
Howard Beach  xi, xii, 20–24, 26–29
*Huckleberry Finn*  105
*Human Events*  78
humanism, Christian  33, 34, 35
humanism, secular  33, 34, 35, 156
humanitarian  38
humanity  34, 44, 45, 46, 54, 70, 158
human life  54, 73
*Human Life Review*  165
human needs  39, 43, 46

humor 123, 132, 135
Humphrey, Hubert 3
Hunt, H.L. 101

## I

Iago 81, 130, 136
ideologies, ideology 4, 9, 10, 23, 26, 29, 33, 34, 40, 41, 43, 46, 49, 64, 82, 101, 108, 156, 159, 160, 162
illiteracy 50
immanentization of the eschaton 86
imperialism 41, 46
*In Bare Ruined Choirs* 84
Incarnation 34
India 10, 83
individualism 56, 85, 86
individual rights 86
infanticide 156, 157, 158
*in loco parentis* 11
insecticide 16
insensitivity 26, 60
investigative journalism 26, 52
Iron Curtain 30, 38, 160
Iron Law 36
IRS 79
Islam 53
isolationist 37
Israel, Israeli 22, 23, 42

## J

Jackson, Jesse 65
Jaffa, Harry 133
Jagger, Mick 112, 114–116
James, Henry 117, 133
Jaszi, Peter 138
Jefferson Airplane 15
Jesus 65, 125, 126, 127, 142
*Jesus of Nazareth* 125, 127
Jew(s), Jewish, Judaism 23, 25, 43, 47, 66, 75, 104, 105, 132, 163
jingoism 96
Joachim of Flora 33
John Birch Society 101

John Paul II 72, 73
Johnson, Dr. 2, 49, 51, 60, 68
Johnson, Eric 148
Johnson, Lyndon B. 1, 26, 149
Jones, Ernest 129, 136
Jonestown 25
Jonson, Ben 118, 121, 123
Joplin, Janis xi, 15, 18
Jordan, Michael 154
journalism xi, 4, 5, 6, 24, 26, 52, 55
journalist xii, 5, 6, 24, 55, 85, 87, 94
Joyce, James 140
Julius Caesar 103, 111
justice 43, 46, 87–89, 136, 154

# K

Kalem, T.E. 135
Kant, Immanuel 22
Keller, Helen 115
Kempton, Murray 21
Kendall, Willmoore 2, 13, 66, 79, 80, 85
Kennedy, David M. 9
Kennedy, Edward 72
Kennedy, John F. 1
Kenner, Hugh 50
Kent 72, 74
Kerrison, Ray 21
KGB 36, 38
Khomeini 42, 53, 55, 91
Kilpatrick, James Jackson 79
Kiner, Ralph 150
*King Lear*: see Lear
King, Corretta Scott 42, 159
King, Larry L. 84
King, Martin Luther 28, 65
Kingfish Stevens 108
Kirk, Russell 79, 123, 132
Klan 22
knowledge 10, 29, 71, 105, 119, 152
Koch, Mayor Ed 21, 39
Koop, Everett 156, 157

Koufax, Sandy 149
Kourdakov, Sergei 38
Krafft-Ebing 8
Kreeger, David Lloyd 138
Kremlin 96
Kristol, Irving 33
Kung 35
Kunstler, William 48

# L

labels 46
Larson, Terry 149
Lear 8, 103, 129, 130, 136, 140
Leavis, F.R. 129, 136
leftist 14, 16, 41, 45, 48
left-wing 5, 25, 40
Left, the 55, 101, 109
Legion of Decency 100
Leigh, Vivien 135
Lenin 50, 94, 98
Leontes 8
Lewis, C.S. 11, 80, 108, 127, 132, 158
Lewis, Wyndham 79
Liberace 24
liberal(s), liberalism xi, xiii, 2, 3, 4, 5, 13, 18, 24, 26, 27, 36, 37, 44, 47, 51, 53, 59, 60, 64, 66, 69, 70, 71, 74, 75, 76, 77, 79, 84, 89, 90, 92, 93, 94, 95, 97, 98, 101–106, 107, 108, 109, 110, 113, 133, 141–144, 159–162
liberal agenda 47
liberation 3, 6, 12, 14, 46
libertarian, libertarianism 5, 13, 43, 100, 159
libertine, libertinism 63
liberty 2, 49, 50, 132, 133
liberty and literacy 50
*Life* 17, 18, 30
Lightfoot, Gordon 113
Lincoln 28
*Lion, the Witch and the Wardrobe, The* 127
literacy 49, 50
Littlefeather, Sacheen 64, 67
living document 47

Locke 49
logic 10, 25, 48, 50, 97, 151, 155
Looney, John Thomas 117
Lord Burghley 119
*Losing Ground* 22
Lou Grant 109
Lourdes 25
love xi, 2, 7, 8, 9, 10, 12, 15, 18, 19, 58, 74, 85, 90, 100, 105, 108, 111, 123, 126, 127, 128, 134, 136
Lovelace, Linda 65, 66
Lukacs, John 50
Luther 4, 28, 65

# M

*Machiavellians, The* 98
Maday, Bob xvi
Madison Avenue 9
*Making It* 84
*Manchild in the Promised Land* 84
Manhattan 39, 56
Manifest Destiny 89
Mantle, Mickey 148, 151
marijuana 16, 115
Maris, Roger 149, 152
marriage 9, 11, 115, 161
martyrdom 101
Marxism, Marxist 37, 41, 123, 144
Mary Tyler Moore 109
Mass ix, 72, 73, 90
mass media 14, 36, 51, 52, 55, 56, 60, 143, 157
maverick 47, 48, 161
McCarthy, Joe, Senator Joseph McCarthy 99
McCarthy, Mary 84
McDonald, Country Joe 16
McGovern, George 33
McGriff, Fred 150
McLain, Denny 149
McLuhan, Professor 132
Mead, Margaret 71
media ix, xi, xii, 5, 14, 20, 22–27, 30, 36, 38, 40, 45, 49, 51–56, 60, 77, 91, 95, 96, 101, 103, 109, 143, 157, 159, 160

Edwin Meese  25, 26
*Memories of a Catholic Girlhood*  84
*Memoirs of a Dissident Publisher*  78
*Men at Work*  153
Mencken, H.L.  48
*Merchant of Venice*  104, 110
messianism  87
Meyer, Frank  79, 85, 86, 87
*Midsummer Night's Dream, A*  135
Mikan, George  154
Miller, Arthur  42
Milton  2, 49, 61, 118
minorities  39, 69, 106, 143
miracle  22, 25, 84, 125, 126, 132, 142
Mitchell, Joni  113
Mitchell, Kevin  150
modern, modernity  10, 11, 12, 33, 34, 49, 50, 59, 72, 82, 103, 104, 133, 136, 140, 141, 142, 144, 145, 150, 158
Molnar, Thomas  33, 34, 35
monarchist, monarchy  5
Monroe, Marilyn  61
Monroe, Vaughn  111
Montagu, Ashley  58
moral, morality  xii, xiii, 4, 6, 7, 8, 9, 11, 14, 22, 23, 30, 55, 56, 60, 62, 63, 81, 82, 83, 94, 97, 100, 101, 105, 108, 112, 123, 153, 154, 157, 158, 161
moral traditions  11
Morley, Felix  78, 79
Mozart  78, 135
*Much Ado About Nothing*  123
Muldaur, Maria  111
Murray, Charles  22
music, musician  xvii, 16, 64, 78, 94, 103, 111, 112, 113, 136, 153, 159
Muslims  13
Mussolini  103, 133, 136
*Mysterious William Shakespeare, The*  139

# N

Nader, Ralph  95
Narnia  127
*National Enquirer*  24

National League 150
*National Review, NR* iii, v, vi, ix, xi, xii, xv, xvi, xvii, xviii, 1–3, 51, 85, 99
*Natural, The* 152
nature 2, 9, 13, 35, 51, 89, 100, 111, 113
Nazis, Nazism 36, 43, 134
NBC 55
Newfield, Jack 21
Newman, John Henry 1, 28, 142
New Hampshire 93, 139
New Jersey 22
*New Republic* 21
*Newsweek* 5, 21, 27, 128
*New York Daily News* 3
*New York Review of Books, The* 82
*New York Times, The* xii, 21, 22, 24, 25, 28, 41, 44, 45, 52, 55, 69, 70, 71, 104, 138, 160
NFL 153
Nicholas of Cusa 34
nihilism 34, 109, 113
*Nixon Agonistes* 89
Nock, Albert Jay 86
Notre Dame University 59, 60
nuclear arms race 40, 43
nuclear freeze 39, 41, 94, 159, 160
nuclear holocaust 39
nuclear weapons 39, 41, 95

# O

objectivity 24, 52, 53, 107, 144
obscene, obscenity 4, 62, 63, 64, 66, 160, 161, 162
Occidentals 106
O'Connor, John J. 55, 104
O'Hair, Madalyn 73
*Odyssey* 90
Oedipus 129, 136
*Official Encyclopedia of Baseball* 149
Ogburn, Jr., Charlton 117, 139
Olivier, Lawrence x, 104, 109, 111, 125, 127, 128, 129, 130, 131, 135, 136
*On Truth* 79

Orientals 106
Orwell, George 98
Othello 8, 128–130, 135, 136
Our Lady of Fatima 90
Oxford x, xii, 117, 119–121, 123, 124, 138–140
Oxfordian(s) 117, 138, 139
Ozzie and Harriet 16

**P**

pacifist 37
paganism 34
Palestinian refugees 79
Panama 92
Papandreou 25
Papp, Joseph 103
*Paradise Lost* 118
Parker, Jim 154
*Partisan Review* 98
Pauley, Jane 40
Paulist Fathers 36
peace 5, 15, 16, 17, 39, 41, 42, 43, 44, 46, 71, 88, 89, 94, 160
Pentagon 25, 41, 43, 159
persecution 2, 25, 37, 89, 95, 144
*Persecutor, The* 38
Peter, Paul, and Mary 42
Philbrick, Herb 36
philosopher(s) 27, 107, 148
Picard, Max 79
Pico della Mirandola 34
Pirates 151
pirates 119
pitcher 149, 150
*Playboy*, Playboy philosophy 61–68, 77, 161
Plummer, Christopher 125
pluralism 48, 143
Plutarch 82
Podhoretz, Norman 1, 21, 84
Poland 73, 74
political 1, 4, 6, 8, 14, 16, 18, 19, 23, 25, 30, 32, 39, 41, 42, 44, 46, 47, 48, 51, 52, 53, 54, 70, 75, 76, 77, 87, 88, 133, 159, 161
political agenda 47
Political Correctness 4

Politically Incorrect 4, 160
political organizations 39, 41, 42, 44, 46
political scientist 75
Polonius 119
pope 4, 72, 73
Pope Leo X 4
popular sentiment 50
population, population policy 4, 11, 88, 133, 139, 150
porn, porno, pornography 8, 47, 48, 55, 62, 63, 161, 162
posthumus 8
Potsdamer, Strasse 31
Pound, Ezra 79, 80
poverty 21, 25
Powell, Robert 125, 126, 127
Pravda 95, 96
pregnancy 10
prejudice(s) 26, 27, 29, 102, 105, 106, 107, 109, 110
Presley, Elvis 111, 112, 113, 115
priest(s) 62, 65, 72, 73, 141, 142, 143, 156
private property 95
profanity 4, 160
progressive, progressivism 4, 5, 6, 11, 25, 26, 28, 29, 45, 46, 101, 102, 133, 154, 160
pro-life movement 6
promiscuity 12
Protestant, Protestantism 76, 109, 142, 158
public opinion 50, 56, 73, 90, 96
Pulitzer Prize 182
Pythagoreans 26

# Q

Queens xi, 20, 27
Quinn, Anthony 125
quotas 47

# R

race xi, 13, 17, 20, 27, 28, 34, 40, 43, 70, 71, 106, 107, 156, 158
racial, racism xii, 4, 20, 21, 22, 27, 29, 43, 47, 59, 60, 69, 70, 85, 92, 107, 112, 154, 160
racially-motiviated 20
Rand, Ayn 82

rape 9, 162
Raspberry, William 21
Rather, Dan 24, 94, 95, 96
reactionary, reactionaries iv, 4, 5, 6, 9, 25, 26, 58, 59, 123
*Reader's Digest* 3
Reagan, Ronald xii, 6, 20, 21, 22, 39, 40, 41, 43, 45, 92–95, 159, 160
Redd Foxx 108
Reed, John 10
re-education 12
Regnery, Henry 78, 79, 80
religion xvii, 4, 12, 23, 33, 37, 44, 49, 59, 95, 102, 103, 141, 157, 160
religious bigotry 102
Renaissance 11, 33, 34
revenge 104
Rhodesia xii, 97
*Richard III* 129, 135, 140
Richards, Keith 115
right-wing 5, 39, 86, 102
Right, the xii, 36, 55, 85, 86, 101, 109
Ritter, Lawrence 154
Robinson, Jackie 28
rock xi, 15, 18, 95, 111–115
Rogers, Will 141
Rogue 61
Rolling Stones 15, 114–116
Romans 30, 123
*Romeo and Juliet* 8
Ronstadt, Linda 42
Roosevelt, Eleanor 2, 3
*Roots* 69, 70, 71
Rosary 73
Rose, Pete 154
Rosse, Dick 30, 31, 32
Rothman, Stanley 83
Rowan, Carl 21
Rusher, Bill 85
Russell (Bertrand) and Whitehead (Albert North) 2
Russia 48, 88, 90
Ruth, Babe 150, 154

# S

sabermetrics  150
sacrament  142
Salinger, J.D.  111
*Sanford and Son*  108
San Francisco  8
Sanger, Margaret  9, 10, 74
Sartre  34
Saul  65
Schaeffer, Francis  156, 157
Scheider, Roy  43
Schlesinger  3
school prayer  47
Scully, Matthew  xv
Second Amendment  47
secular humanism  33, 34, 35, 156
Seeger, Pete  42
self-fulfillment  142, 144
Seneca  34
sex, sexism, sexist, sexual, sexuality  xi, 4, 6, 7, 8–10, 12–16, 27, 41, 58–60, 68, 72, 106, 130, 146, 157, 160, 162
Shafarevich, Igor  12, 13
Shah of Iran  6
Shakespeare  iv, xii, xv, xvi, 1, 8, 82, 85, 103–105, 109–110, 117–124, 128–133, 135–136, 138–140, 162, 163, 165
*Shakespeare Revealed in Oxford's Letters*  139
Shaw, Bernard  82
Sheen, Martin  37
Shylock  104, 105, 109, 136
Simon, Carly  111, 113
*Single Issues*  iv, 165
Sixties  19, 30, 58, 59, 87, 107, 112, 113, 141, 149, 156
slave labor  88
slavery, slaves  5, 30, 69, 70, 71
Smith College  27
Smith, Maggie  130
*Sobran's: The Real News of the Month*  iv, xvii, 165
social engineering  10
socialism, socialist  5, 6, 7, 8, 10, 11, 12, 13–14, 25, 30, 39, 41, 43, 44, 45, 46, 48, 53, 82–83, 92, 94, 158, 160
*Socialist Phenomenon, The*  12

social justice  43, 46, 154
social power  86
society  xii, xvii, 10, 11, 12, 13, 19, 21, 26, 28, 29, 49, 54, 58, 62, 64, 66, 67, 70, 82, 84, 88, 89, 101, 132–133, 139, 153
sociologist, sociology  28, 29
Socrates  66, 109
Solzhenitsyn  109
sonnets  xii, 103, 118–120
Sophocles  34, 118
soul(s)  xvi, xix, 8, 9, 61, 104, 115, 133, 153
South, Southern  10, 13, 25, 36, 69
South Africa  13, 25
Southern states  10
sovereign will  12
Soviet(s), Soviet Bloc, Soviet Union  25, 36, 37, 38, 40, 42, 46, 48, 54, 71, 79, 83, 87, 88, 89, 94, 95, 96, 160
Springer, Axel  31
Stalin  2, 98
Stanford  4
Starr, Roger  82
state(s)  xii, 3, 7, 10, 11, 12, 13, 30, 35, 51, 63, 76, 83, 86–89, 100, 103, 133, 158
Steinbrenner, George  151
Stengel, Casey  153
stereotype(s), stereotyping  6, 19, 29, 56, 69, 70, 100, 105, 106, 107, 108–110
sterilization  133, 157
St. Louis Browns  151–152
St. Martin de Porres Lay Dominican Community  vi, xix
Stevens, John Paul  138
*Stoic Comedians, The*  50
Stratford, Stratfordian  117, 121, 123, 138, 139
Strawberry, Darryl  150
strident  45, 46
subversion  37, 67
supernatural  74, 143
Supreme Court  14, 62, 66, 117, 138, 154, 161
Sweden  13, 156

# T

taboo(s) 4, 28, 29, 30, 58, 60, 82, 101, 104, 144, 157, 160
Tacelli, S.J., Fr. Ronald xviii
talk shows 58
Taylor, James 42
Taylor, Zack 151
Teheran 55, 92
television 38, 45, 54, 58, 70, 100, 102, 108, 127
*Tempest, The* 103, 121, 140
Tennyson 7
*The Boys From Brazil* 36
theocracy 5, 86
Third World 6, 43, 53, 83, 92
Thirties 136, 153
thought control 101
*Three's Company* 100
Tigers 149, 151
*Time After Time* 8
*Time* magazine 17, 21, 135, 156
Titus 128, 129
Titus Andronicus 128
tolerance 71, 76, 109
totalitarian 45, 50, 54, 66, 83, 88, 89
Townshend, Pete 16
tradition(s), traditional, traditionalism 11, 14, 34, 35, 46, 84, 88, 101, 103, 104, 109, 113, 133, 138, 141–144, 149, 157
traditionalists 142, 143
traits 106, 107, 108
trendiness 38, 84, 85, 114
Troilus 8
Troilus and Cressida 118, 120
Trotsky, Trotskyist xii, 86, 98
Tunis, John R. 149, 152
Tussman, Joseph 107
*TV Guide* 3
Twain, Mark 87, 105, 117
Twenties 150
typecasting 5
tyranny 37, 71, 96

## U

Ulbricht, Walter  31
Ulysses  48
unborn  11, 34, 73, 110
underground Church  84
United Nations, U.N.  3, 39, 42, 53
Universal Press Syndicate  165
unpatriotism  55
Updike, John  67, 154
U.S. Civil Rights Commission  108
Ustinov  125
utopia, utopian  iv, 8, 18, 33, 34, 49, 155

## V

Van Cliburn  16
Van den Haag, Ernest  2, 81, 82
Van Horne, Harriett  3
Vanessa  72, 74
Vatican  132, 141
Vatican II, Second Vatican Council  132, 141
Veeck, Bill  151
Vergil  34
Vietnam  26, 88, 92, 95, 144
*Village Voice*  21, 43
virginity  61
Vivaldi  104
Voegelin, Eric  33, 86
*Volk*  12
Vree, Dale  83

## W

*Wall Street Journal*  3
Wallace, Henry  98
war(s)  xii, 8, 26, 37, 40, 41, 42, 43, 44, 46, 70, 77, 79, 86, 88, 89, 90, 94, 95, 104, 113, 151, 152, 159, 160
warmongers  11, 41
*War of the Worlds*  105
*Washington Post*  xvii, 23, 27, 30, 42
*Washington Star*  31
Watergate  26, 92
Watson, James  156

Watt, James  25, 26
Wavy Gravy  16
Weiss, George  151
Welles, Orson  40, 44–45, 67, 105
Wells, H.G.  8
West, decline of  53
West, the  xiii, 2, 4, 7, 28, 38, 45, 53, 54, 70, 73, 83, 96, 97, 98, 144, 156, 158, 160
Western culture  4
Westerner, Westerners  23, 50, 53, 70
*What Ever Happened to the Human Race?*  156, 158
Whig  4, 141
*Whig Interpretation of History, A*  4
white guilt  69, 70
Whitehead  2
*White Sox Year Book, The*  79
Whitman, Walt  117, 123
Who, The  15, 16
Wicker, Tom  71
Wilde, Oscar  7
Wilkins, Roger  21, 22, 69, 70, 71
Will, George  153
William of Ockham  34
Williams, Raymond  54
Williams, Ted  146
Williamson, Bruce  63
Wills, Garry  65, 70, 71, 84, 85
Winter, Johnny  15
*Winter's Tale, The*  119
Wolfe, Tom  42, 64
Woodstock, Woodstockian  xi, 15–19, 85
Word, The  126
World Series  115, 149, 152
World War II  77, 86, 151

# Y

Yankees  148, 149, 151
Yasgur, Max  15, 17
Ypsilanti, Michigan  146, 165

# Z

Zefirelli, Franco  125
Zimbabwe  92

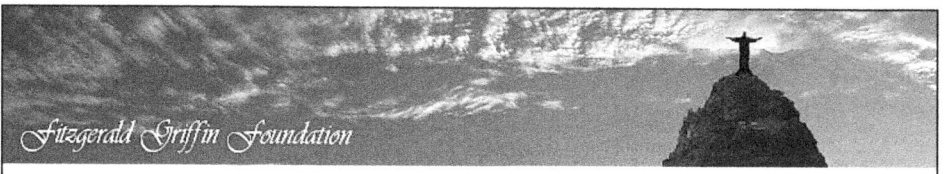

## Fitzgerald Griffin Foundation

Joe Sobran encouraged the founding of the Fitzgerald Griffin Foundation in 2003. His extraordinary talent was discovered by William F. Buckley, who brought him to *National Review* magazine in 1971. He wrote bylined and unsigned pieces for the magazine for 23 years. This volume is but a sampling of his work.

From its origin, FGF saw the need to promote ideas that used to be mainstream in American culture but were becoming counter-cultural or even brushed aside as being old-fashioned or not important, such as belief in God, Christianity, religious liberty, the sanctity of life from conception until natural death, the principles of a just war, the threat of totalitarianism, creeping socialism and the welfare state; the sanctity of marriage between one man and one woman, and the importance of the founding documents of our country, the Declaration of Independence and the Constitution. The writings of Joseph Sobran match our mission in every one of these areas.

A major goal of FGF is to promote and defend our Western Christian heritage. We strive to educate our fellow citizens by providing well-written books, essays, and materials – as well as sponsoring lectures and conferences. With the publication of the second edition of the collection of Sobran's *National Review* columns, we are trying to do more than just preserve his legacy. We are hoping to inspire readers to think and explore the many ideas presented herein.

Mrs. Fran Griffin, O.P., Founder and President

### Board of Directors
Miss Nona Aguilar, New York City
Rev. Bartholomew de la Torre, O.P., Mexicali, Mexico
Jean-Francois Orsini, O.P., Ph.D., Washington, D.C.
Charles Mills, Esq., Front Royal, Virginia

Fitzgerald Griffin Foundation
344 Maple Avenue West, #281, Vienna, Virginia 22180-5612
877-726-0358 • www.fgfBooks.com • fgf@fgfBooks.com

Made in the USA
Monee, IL
24 October 2021